MONADNOCK
ORIGINALS

MONADNOCK
ORIGINALS

COLORFUL CHARACTERS FROM NEW HAMPSHIRE'S QUIET CORNER

ALAN F. RUMRILL

THE
History
PRESS

Published by The History Press
Charleston, SC
www.historypress.com

All images are courtesy of the Historical Society of Cheshire County.

First published 2023

Manufactured in the United States

ISBN 9781467152648

Library of Congress Control Number: 2022949526

Notice: The information in this book is true and complete to the best of our knowledge. It is offered without guarantee on the part of the author or The History Press. The author and The History Press disclaim all liability in connection with the use of this book.

CONTENTS

ACKNOWLEDGEMENTS

O nce again, I find myself acknowledging the board of trustees of the Historical Society of Cheshire County for encouraging my use of the society's collections, as well as my work hours, to develop and tell stories of the Monadnock region. This book would not have been possible without the extensive archival collection maintained by the historical society. All of the photographs used in the book are from the collections of the historical society. A special thank-you goes to the many donors who continue to add to the society's collections so that this history can be shared with a wider audience.

I am grateful to Jenna Carroll for her assistance in formatting the text of the manuscript for this work. My research assistant (and daughter), Jennifer Rumrill, spent many hours researching these historic topics. I thank her for so much behind-the-scenes work.

This research was made easier thanks to the efforts of a group of organizations that recently partnered to digitize almost 150 years of the *New Hampshire Sentinel* and *Keene Sentinel* newspapers. The Historical Society of Cheshire County, Keene Public Library, New Hampshire State Library and the *Keene Sentinel* itself collaborated to sponsor a project to digitize the *Sentinel* from 1799 to 1945, making the extensive files of the newspaper fully searchable for the first time.

I must express my gratitude to the Monadnock Broadcasting Group and the *Keene Sentinel* for airing and printing so many of these stories in the first place. Without their confidence in my ability to find and compose stories of the region, the historical society would not have been able to share them with such a wide audience. I appreciate their years of support. My thanks also go to Dan Mitchell, my contact at Monadnock Broadcasting Group, for encouraging the development of this book.

Finally, I am grateful to the local historians who devoted so many years of their time to saving the historic details of some of these stories so they would not be forgotten. Salma Hale (1787–1866), William S. Briggs (1817–1901), Samuel Wadsworth (1846–1931), Clifford Wilbur (1884–1962), Marjorie W. Smith (1925–2021) and David R. Proper (1933–2014) were a few of those who labored diligently to gather, protect and share the region's history as a labor of love. I dedicate this book to them and hope that someday my name might be considered worthy of addition to this list.

INTRODUCTION

"The Legend of Granite Lake," included in this volume, recounts a fanciful tale of a Native American maiden who inhabited a small rocky island in one of the Monadnock region's dozens of lakes and ponds. Native Americans lived in this region for about thirteen thousand years before European settlers arrived in the area three hundred years ago. Once those settlers arrived, the region changed. Technology and land use have had a major impact on southwest New Hampshire over the past three centuries.

The landscape here was cleared for agriculture and then for industry in the eighteenth and nineteenth centuries. Despite these changes, large-scale development bypassed the area in the twentieth century. The Monadnock region today is a quiet locale blessed with natural beauty and well-preserved history and traditions. The region is, in fact, often referred to as New Hampshire's "quiet corner."

The lack of development resulted in a region that is home to many well-preserved quintessential New England villages. Consequently, southwest New Hampshire has also been dubbed the "Currier & Ives Corner" of the state in an effort to attract heritage tourists. Finally, the widespread agricultural and industrial use of the land has decreased or become more environmentally responsible, resulting in vast tracts of forest dotted with lakes and ponds and crisscrossed by countless rivers and streams. This natural beauty, much of it available for public enjoyment, has made the region an ecotourism destination.

The forty communities located in the southwest corner of New Hampshire experienced the history outlined above, proceeding from the story of the region's Native Americans, through the expansion of agriculture, industry and tourism. Furthermore, the residents on the land that now make up these communities have always felt a physical and spiritual connection to the region's namesake mountain and geological focal point—Mount Monadnock.

For the past ninety-five years, the Historical Society of Cheshire County has focused on its mission to preserve and share the history of this unique region. The society has 300,000 historic items in its collections. We like to say that each item tells a story, so we have 300,000 stories to share. We find that residents of the region are attracted to stories from the past. They help people relate to the past and comfortably fit into the fabric of the region, whether they are newcomers or their families have been here for generations.

The staff of the organization shares many stories through its schedule of 150 programs presented annually. Perhaps the most effective way of sharing these stories with a wide audience, however, has been through the weekly newspaper and radio features that the staff has prepared for the past thirty-seven years. The tales in this volume were previously shared via radio or newsprint but have never been compiled in one manuscript.

This work includes tales of successful businesses, famous folks, military heroes, dastardly criminals and frightening disasters. An effort has been made, however, to focus on three specific topics that often get little attention but offer some of the most compelling insight into the identity of the region. The stories of early days in the area illustrate the challenges that long-ago residents faced in an effort to persist in the wilderness. Stories of empowered women from the quiet corner share the experiences of strong women who were often not at all quiet. Finally, the tales of local Yankee characters illustrate the individuality, edginess and strong disposition of the residents of the Monadnock region.

We hope that this small selection of the historical society's 300,000 stories will entertain readers. We also hope an understanding of the past will help them recognize why the area is the way it is today—a quiet yet vibrant region that cherishes its unique history. Finally, we hope these historic vignettes might help readers discover their own place in our local history.

Chapter 1

EARLY DAYS IN THE MONADNOCK REGION

PACKERSFIELD, NEW HAMPSHIRE

The town of Packersfield in Cheshire County was formed in 1774. It was named for Thomas Packer, the high sheriff of Portsmouth, who was one of the largest landowners in the new town. Packer promised to give some of his property to the town in return for having the township named in his honor. He did indeed give two lots to the son of Breed Batchelder, the first settler of Packersfield. According to the town historian, however, no more land was ever given by Packer, and the townspeople became very upset with him.

In 1777, the townspeople petitioned to have the name of the town changed to Sullivan. The state legislature would not allow the change, however. Three years later, in 1780, the legislature passed an act suspending all property tax payments by Packer because of a problem with his father's will. Because Packer owned so much land in Packersfield, this was a great burden on the town finances. The selectmen petitioned the legislature for relief from this tax problem. This nonpayment of taxes undoubtedly added to the hard feelings the town had for the Packer family.

Years passed, but the townspeople never forgot their early unhappiness with Thomas Packer. Another petition to change the name of Packersfield was sent to the legislature by the townspeople in 1813. This petition was approved in 1814, and the name of Packersfield ceased to exist. Following the thirty-five-year grudge against Thomas Packer, the town of Packersfield was renamed Nelson in honor of British naval hero Lord Horatio Nelson.

Jaffrey's Long-Lived Minister

Laban Ainsworth was born in Woodstock, Connecticut, in July 1757. At the age of eighteen years, he entered Dartmouth College in the summer of 1775. As young Ainsworth began his college career at Dartmouth, the townspeople of Jaffrey, New Hampshire, some eighty miles to the south, were raising the framework for their new meetinghouse, which still stands on the town common today.

Ainsworth received his first degree from Dartmouth in 1778 and then continued to earn a master of arts degree in 1781. On commencement day that year, a committee from Jaffrey met with Ainsworth in Hanover and invited him to preach at the new meetinghouse in Jaffrey. The meetinghouse, although not yet completed, was suitable for services, but the new church body had not yet hired a full-time minister. The residents of Jaffrey approved of what they heard from the young minister. He was called to become the full-time minister in July and was ordained as Jaffrey's first settled minister in December 1782.

This ordination began a decades-long relationship between preacher, church and town. This was a time when a call to preach at a New England Congregational church was viewed as a potential lifetime appointment unless some problem arose between the minster and his congregation. Ainsworth did indeed remain in the town for the remainder of his long career and his long life.

Laban Ainsworth became involved in the town's social, political and economic life, as well as its religion. He farmed his land, was librarian of the Jaffrey Social Library and was elected to the state legislature. He married Mary Minot in 1787, and the couple had two children, a son and a daughter. The family lived in the large home they built within sight of the meetinghouse.

In 1832, the minister celebrated his 50th anniversary as minister of the Jaffrey church. Although a junior pastor was installed to assist in the pulpit that year, Ainsworth continued his duties. The town celebrated his 100th birthday in July 1857. Eight months later, he passed away. Jaffrey's Laban Ainsworth had completed more than 75 years as the town's minister, the longest-serving Congregational minister in history.

Patty Ward Remembered

Patty Ward was the daughter of Reuben and Sarah Ward, early settlers of Marlborough, New Hampshire. The Wards first arrived in Marlborough in 1774. They had journeyed from Marlborough, Massachusetts, with two young daughters, ages one and two years.

Reuben Ward cleared his farmland and soon became involved in the town's social and political affairs. He was the town hog reeve and was on the church council, school district committee and was a founding member of the Marlborough Social Library. His farm was prosperous, and he was considered one of the wealthiest men in town.

The subject of our story, however, is young Patty Ward. She was born in April 1790, the ninth of eleven children of Reuben and Sarah. Most of Patty's brothers and sisters went on to lead long and successful lives, with several moving west into New York State.

The late eighteenth century was a time when there were more perils present in the American household than we experience today. Household accidents were all too common. House fires ignited often because open flames were commonplace; candles were used for light, and open fireplaces were used for heating and cooking. The use of those fireplaces for cooking meant that boiling liquids and hot food were also near at hand.

Young Patty fell victim to such an accident. In November 1795, at five and a half years of age, just as she began her schooling and began making childhood friends, she died a sad death. To perpetuate her memory, the tale of her tragic passing was inscribed on her gravestone. Patty Ward has not been forgotten. Her stone still stands in Marlborough's Meetinghouse Cemetery. Her epitaph reads as follows:

> *By boiling cyder she was slain,*
> *Whilst less than six of age,*
> *Then her exquisite racking pain*
> *Removed her from the stage.*
> *But her immortal spirit went*
> *To the Almighty King,*
> *Where all the Godly ones are sent,*
> *The praise of God to sing.*

THE FIRST WASHINGTON

The town of Camden, New Hampshire, was granted in the late 1760s in honor of Baron Camden, an English friend of New Hampshire's colonial governor. The inhabitants of Camden petitioned the New Hampshire legislature for formal incorporation as a township in the autumn of 1776.

The thirteen colonies had recently declared their independence from Britain and formed the United States of America. One of the first acts of the new state legislature of New Hampshire was to approve the incorporation of this new town in the southwestern part of the state.

Meshech Ware, the state's first governor, recommended that the new town be named Washington, in honor of General George Washington, who was leading the new country's troops against the British in the battle for independence. Consequently, on December 9, 1776, the town of Washington, New Hampshire, was formed.

Twenty-three other states subsequently named towns in honor of the country's Revolutionary leader and first president. Many other natural features and political subdivisions were named in his honor, from lakes, mountains and bays to the state of Washington and the District of Columbia. However, the people of Washington, New Hampshire, named in December 1776, claim that their town was the first place in the United States to be named in honor of George Washington.

THE CHASE TAVERN

From the middle of the eighteenth century through the early decades of the nineteenth century, Keene was the home of many taverns. When people traveled by horseback or stagecoach, they needed to be able to stop often to warm themselves by the tavern fireplaces. One of the most popular in Keene was the Chase Tavern on the Third New Hampshire Turnpike. The tavern was built in 1794 by Stephen Chase. The house remains today at 712 Court Street as a wonderful example of the colonial architecture of Keene's early days.

Taverns were very different from the hotels of today. One person traveling through Keene in 1800 kept a journal of his travels. He stayed at the Chase Tavern. His journal entry for that day gives us a delightful view of tavern life more than two hundred years ago. The entry reads:

Stephen Chase built his tavern on Court Street in Keene in 1794.

Chase's Tavern where we lodged last night is a good tavern in many respects. Good attendance, but all sorts put up there. We lodged in a large chamber with 3 beds in it; then up came 4 creatures after we got to bed who were as noisy, profane mortals as my ears were ever the witness of. Their obscene discourse and filthy stories were exceeding burdensome. They appear to be hardened inconsiderate wretches. We said nothing to them, arose early, paid our reckoning, mounted, and pursued on our journey.

It was indeed common for unacquainted travelers to share the same room or even the same bed. A fire in the room cost extra, and so did a bath. Chase's Tavern in Keene remained popular for many years; as late as 1825, it had the reputation of being "a good comfortable place, and quite clear of lice."

Buss Family Farm

The story of the life of David Buss, born just before the outbreak of the Revolutionary War, offers a detailed illustration of life in the wilderness of the Monadnock region in the late eighteenth and early nineteenth centuries.

David grew up in the town of Marlborough, New Hampshire. He had very little formal education because his labor on the farm could not be spared so that he could attend school. When he reached the age of twenty-one, he left home to seek his fortune. He took a job that paid eight dollars per month, plus board. After seven years, he had saved several hundred dollars and left his employer to start a family and a farm of his own.

In 1803, David married Anna Jones of Dublin. The couple's first child was born the following year, and they moved to Marlow in 1805. It took David two days to travel from Marlborough to Marlow, pulling his belongings behind a yoke of oxen. David and Anna moved in with the family of Anna's sister and bought a 118-acre piece of wilderness land in the town. David cleared 4 acres and built a twenty-two-by-twenty-eight-foot house with three rooms and a large pantry; the small family moved into their new home in the winter of 1806. David then built a barn and continued to clear land and increase his crops. The farm produced almost all that was needed to feed and clothe the family.

As the family grew, so did the farm. David constructed other outbuildings and, after the family grew to eight children, added two rooms onto the house. He soon built a larger barn to accommodate his increased crops and growing number of livestock. David and his sons cleared more land every year for twenty-eight years in a row. They eventually built a stone wall that encircled the entire property.

The entire family helped on the farm, which was soon home to thirty to fifty sheep, twenty to thirty cattle, eight milk cows and several pigs. The Busses sold excess cheese, butter and pork to earn some cash to buy what they could not make themselves. The local shoemaker came in the fall to make boots and shoes for the children to wear to school. This was followed by the seamstress, who made new clothes for the coming school term. The school was one and a half miles from the house, and the children walked to school in all kinds of weather.

David Buss walked into Marlow at the age of thirty and fashioned a farm from the wilderness to support his large family. His children all went out into the world before David passed away at age seventy, after forty years on his neat and successful Marlow farm. Forty years after David's death, the Buss farm had reverted to forest once again, like so many thousands of others across southwest New Hampshire.

Chapter 2

BUSINESS, INDUSTRY, INVENTORS

Monadnock Mineral Spring

With the recent revival of the spring water industry, it is interesting to note that the Monadnock region has been the home of several commercial mineral springs over the years. Perhaps the first of these to be used for financial gain was the Monadnock Mineral Spring in Jaffrey.

The water of this spring contained iron and sulfur and was believed to have medicinal value long before John Joslin decided to capitalize on it in 1804. During that year, Joslin purchased the spring and two and a half acres around it for $100. In 1805, the state legislature incorporated the Monadnock Mineral Spring with Joslin and five other Jaffrey residents as the proprietors. These men built a house beside the spring, and in 1808, Joslin was licensed to operate the Monadnock Mineral Spring House, a resort hotel where visitors would use the water to regain their health.

Eight years later, Dr. Freeman Dana, a chemistry professor from Harvard, visited the spring while on a trip to Mount Monadnock. He tested the water during his visit. He then published a report stating that the water did indeed contain iron, but it was scarcely enough to justify the title "mineral water."

This report undoubtedly hurt business, but Joslin was not ready to give up yet. He found another use for the spring. Yellow ochre, a mineral oxide, built up around the hole where the spring flowed from the earth. By 1823, Joslin had sold thirty tons of this ochre in Boston to be used in the coloring of paint. John Joslin sold the Monadnock Mineral Spring House in 1824 and retired to Marlborough.

THE CHESHIRE HOUSE

The corner of Main Street and Central Square in Keene was long the home of taverns and hotels. The Lion and Brazen Ball Tavern opened there in 1788. It burned in 1822 and was replaced by a large brick hotel that was cleverly named the Phoenix Hotel, which also burned fourteen years later.

From the ashes of the Phoenix arose the most famous hotel in Keene's history. The Cheshire House was built by a group of Keene businessmen in 1837. The hotel was already well known in the region when Henry Pond purchased the business and enlarged it to eighty guest rooms. In the 1880s, a new east wing was built along Roxbury Street, enlarging the hotel even more.

With the purchase of the hotel by Charles Hartwell in 1891, the Cheshire House began to build its reputation beyond the Monadnock region. He renovated and updated the business, adding bay windows in the south wing, installing closets and new bathrooms and adding all new carpets and furniture. The hotel was soon drawing guests from across New England and beyond. The hotel's restaurant could seat two hundred diners. Room rates were $2.50 per day or $3.00 with a private bath.

Keene's famed Cheshire House hotel opened in 1837. Among its many guests were Thomas Edison, Henry Ford, President Calvin Coolidge and President William Howard Taft.

Hartwell was followed by Judson Reynolds, the best known of the Cheshire House owners. He operated the hotel for more than thirty years. He welcomed many rich and famous guests, including Thomas Edison, Henry Ford, President Calvin Coolidge and President William Howard Taft, who made a speech from the second-floor balcony in 1912. At one time, Reynolds declined to host a party for the Rockefeller family because it would have interfered with the regular 6:00 p.m. dinner schedule.

The Cheshire House menu was also famous, offering dozens of options at every meal. Unusual offerings included fried bananas, pickled lamb's tongue and fried pig's feet, calf brains and cod tongues. By 1933, the dinner menu included more than fifty items and eight- to ten-course meals. It was during that year that Reynolds decided to retire.

The hotel's final dinner was served on New Year's Eve 1933. The menu included twenty-two selections of seafood as well as roast turkey, goose, sirloin steak, New England boiled dinner, thirteen vegetables, six cheeses and several desserts. Four days later, the furnishings, silver, dishes and other interior accessories were sold at auction. The hotel was quickly torn down and replaced by a one-story business block that still stands on the corner of Main and Roxbury Streets. The old Cheshire House has been gone for almost a century, but its fame lives on in the city of Keene.

Moses Morse and the Common Pin

Did you realize that it was a former Keene resident whose invention made the common pin widely available to the public? Moses L. Morse, born in Sutton, Massachusetts, in 1781, lived in Keene during the first decade of the nineteenth century. He worked as a watch and clock maker while in Keene.

Morse returned to Massachusetts by 1810. It was during the War of 1812 that Morse, aided by Oliver Hall, devised a machine to produce pins with solid heads. The pin had been invented thousands of years earlier, but prior to Morse's time, pins were made by hand and were rare and expensive. Morse's invention made production quicker so that pins were less expensive and more readily available.

He developed a machine that could make pins with a head attached and could make them much faster than those made by hand. In 1814, he received the first American patent for a pin-making machine.

In June 1815, Morse and three partners received authority from the Massachusetts legislature to incorporate a company known as the Patent Pin

Manufactory "for the purpose of manufacturing pins with solid heads from the wire in one operation." Morse's machine and the manufactory were not a commercial success, however. One contemporary suggested that the pin-making machine exhibited "much mechanical genius" but was too delicate to be truly successful.

Moses Morse passed away in Worcester, Massachusetts, in 1831. One year later, John Howe of Connecticut received another patent for a pin-making machine and began the first truly successful pin-manufacturing company in this country. Howe is remembered today as the father of the American pin-manufacturing industry. Former Keene resident Moses Morse, like so many other contributors to American industrial progress, has been virtually forgotten today.

GRAVES INSTRUMENT COMPANY

One of Cheshire County's more unusual and successful early manufacturing firms was Graves & Company, located in Winchester. Samuel Graves Jr. began the manufacture of musical instruments near his father's farm at West Fairlee, Vermont, in about 1824. By 1830, the company had moved to a four-story mill building alongside the Ashuelot River in Winchester.

Graves & Company produced large numbers of woodwind and brass musical instruments and was the first American company to truly challenge European instruments in the American market. The production of this Winchester factory was larger, and its line of instruments more extensive, than any other American firm before the Civil War.

Samuel Graves and his partners, including two brothers, a cousin and a brother-in-law, worked in Winchester for twenty years. They produced fifes, piccolos, flutes, clarinets, bugles, trumpets, tubas, trombones and other brass instruments. In the mid-1840s, a local news article reported that the Graves instruments were equal to any made in Europe and that the company had difficulty keeping ahead of its orders. By the late 1840s, however, the firm had fallen on hard times, apparently due to a tariff reduction and a fire at the factory.

Graves & Company, the largest musical instrument manufacturing enterprise in the country, closed in 1850 after twenty years in Winchester. The firm moved to Boston the following year, and the Graves family continued to produce musical instruments there until the late 1870s.

Stoddard Glass

Glassblower Joseph Foster established Stoddard's famed glass industry in 1842. The Foster family remained in the glass industry for five generations.

During 1842, glassblower Joseph Foster purchased the glass-making equipment of the recently closed Keene bottle factory and moved the operation to the woods of Stoddard, New Hampshire. He built a small furnace near the house that he purchased there and began to produce bottles for various businesses in the region.

This was the beginning of an industry that would support hundreds of Stoddard residents over the next three decades. Four glass companies came and went. The most successful firm, which was the last to close in 1873, was the South Stoddard Glass Manufacturing Company.

Glass blowing was a skilled profession. Many of the Stoddard blowers learned their trade in Europe before migrating to America. They worked long hours around hot furnaces producing several hundred bottles by hand each day.

These glass houses produced a wide variety of bottles for firms throughout New England and New York, including Dr. Townsend Sarsaparilla and the mineral water spas at Saratoga, New York. All the Stoddard factories made common utilitarian bottles in dark colors, mostly amber and green.

The industry died in Stoddard for several reasons. The Saratoga spas began to decline in the 1860s, and Stoddard could not compete with other glass companies that had cheaper transportation costs. Furthermore, the clear glass that consumers were beginning to demand could not be produced in Stoddard with the raw materials available there.

Manufacturing records indicate that individual companies in the town produced almost one million bottles a year. These sold for about forty cents per dozen. Today's bottle collectors are willing to pay as much as $40,000 or more for a single piece of glass made in the town. The crude but beautiful glass blown in the woods of Stoddard more than 150 years ago is among the most sought-after antique glass in the country today.

THE MONADNOCK MOUNTAIN HOUSE

Mountain resorts came into vogue in the mid-1800s as residents of the growing cities of the eastern United States longed to escape the crowding, pollution and noise of the urban areas, especially during the heat of summer. The era of the grand hotel in Cheshire County truly began with the Mountain House on Mount Monadnock, later to be called the Halfway House. Visitors were coming to the mountain to enjoy the expansive views as early as the 1840s.

In the 1850s, the *New Hampshire Sentinel* suggested that a hotel was needed on Monadnock. Three years later, Moses Cudworth followed this advice and built a house on the mountain where he cared for the horses of day-trippers and took in occasional overnight guests.

Shortly thereafter, the land was sold, and George D. Rice, the new proprietor, went about building a grand new hotel. His three-and-a-half-story Mountain House was opened for business during the season of 1866. That first season was a bright and active one. Rice advertised accommodations for one hundred guests at eight to fourteen dollars weekly, children at half rate. A refreshment stand was built on the summit, where brass bands gave concerts, and on October 2, Luther Richardson of Stoddard and Rachel Tarbox of Sullivan held their wedding on top of the mountain.

The Monadnock Mountain House, located halfway up the region's namesake mountain, hosted lovers of the region's natural landscape.

Tragedy struck at the end of the first season, however. The staff closed the hotel on October 11 and headed down the mountain. As they reached the bottom, they looked back to see the building in flames.

The property was sold, and the new owners built a new hotel during 1868. Over the next ten years, the popularity of the Mountain House grew. The hotel itself also grew as new additions more than tripled the size of the structure. Ralph Waldo Emerson's visit was typical of that of other guests. He arrived by train from Boston at the Troy depot and traveled by coach to the front steps of the hotel. Guests at the grand hotels generally traveled by train and often stayed several weeks or the entire summer. Most of the guests wanted to climb up to the summit, and soon several hiking trails were laid out and marked.

The name was changed to Halfway House in 1916 as the hotel continued longer than many of its counterparts. It was still being used as a summer resort when it burned on the night of April 14, 1954, ending the era of the grand hotel in Cheshire County.

Jacob Estey's Organs

Jacob Estey was born in Hinsdale, New Hampshire, in 1814. When he was four years old, he was adopted by the Steams family of that town. Young Jacob ran away at the age of thirteen and walked to Worcester, where his brother lived. He worked on a farm there and attended Worcester High School. At the age of seventeen, he apprenticed to learn the plumber's trade. Three years later, having saved $200, he walked to Brattleboro, Vermont, and opened a plumbing business.

In 1848, Estey erected a large building for his business. He rented the upper level to the proprietors of a small melodeon factory. Two years later, Estey accepted an interest in the melodeon business in lieu of rent. He purchased the entire business in 1855. Estey soon disposed of his plumbing business and devoted himself exclusively to the manufacture of organs.

The firm had about six employees when he purchased it, but the business rapidly increased. Fire and flood damaged or destroyed the factory buildings on three occasions. Estey rebuilt each time. Following the third disaster, the company purchased sixty acres and erected a new manufacturing facility. The plant eventually contained eight large manufacturing buildings and numerous other related structures.

By the 1880s, the Estey Organ Company was the largest parlor organ factory in the world, employing between five hundred and six hundred people. By 1884, the company had manufactured almost 150,000 organs and sold them around the world. Jacob Estey died in 1890.

The market for parlor organs soon died out as well, and the Estey Organ Company has been gone for many years. The factory buildings in Brattleboro remain today, however, as a memorial to Hinsdale native and organ king Jacob Estey. The Estey Organ Museum is in one of the former factory buildings.

The Cow in the Mud

One afternoon in 1872, Keene businessman John A. Wright was driving along a road south of Keene when he came across a cow stuck in the mud in a bog beside the road. He went to find the neighboring farmer, and the two men went back to the cow and managed to pull it from the mud. As the two men stood talking and watching the cow recover from its harrowing experience, Wright noticed that the dark mud on the cow's legs became lighter and lighter in color as it dried. Wright, being an amateur geologist and familiar with chemistry, was intrigued by the mud. He collected a sample and took it with him to be analyzed.

The analysis determined that the mud from the bog was actually diatomaceous earth, consisting of fossilized remains of diatoms, a type of microscopic hard-shelled algae. Wright was told that the diatomaceous earth had several commercial uses, including polishing metal. The fossils were abrasive enough to polish metal but were so small that they would not scratch it. Realizing that the earth might have value, Wright purchased two acres around the site where the cow had been mired in the mud, near the border of Fitzwilliam and Troy, for $1,000 early in 1873.

Wright began draining the area he had purchased and erected a building sixty feet long to store, dry and prepare the earth for commercial use. It was transported in barrels to the Eagle Hotel in Keene. The earth was sifted and packaged in a back room of the hotel and marketed as a powder used to clean silver.

John A. Wright began to market his cleaning powder by going house to house with a horse and buggy. The *New Hampshire Sentinel* newspaper reported that the powder was "the most valuable polishing powder in the market." This bit of free publicity spread the word even farther, and nearby dealers

John A. Wright, *in top hat*, posed at his diatomaceous earth mining operation soon after forming his silver polish company.

began to stock the powder. The first shipments were delivered from the hotel to the railroad station in a wheelbarrow. Wright was able to introduce the powder to the grand hotels of New Hampshire, Massachusetts and beyond. There was a ready market in those late Victorian period hotels, where large amounts of elaborate silverware were used by the guests.

From this simple beginning, the new J.A. Wright Company combined quality products and a masterful advertising plan to become a world leader in the metal polish industry, selling its products throughout the western hemisphere. J.A. Wright & Co. continued through five generations of family ownership, producing fine metal polishes in Keene until 2006. The company was sold, and the Wright product line is now produced by the Weiman Products Company of Gurnee, Illinois.

MOUNTAIN SPRING BREWERY

With the recent expansion of the number of craft breweries in southwest New Hampshire, it is interesting to look back at the largest commercial brewery in Cheshire County history. In 1877, Alvah Walker of Boston and

Warren Walker and Charles Blake of Bellows Falls formed the partnership of Walker, Blake and Company, with a capital stock of $100,000. The company was to manufacture lager beer near Cold River in Walpole.

The company built a large five-story brick brewery building, sixty feet by forty-two feet in size, copying a model exhibited at the centennial celebration in Philadelphia the previous year. The company's office was headquartered in Bellows Falls.

The owners advertised that the medical profession did not hesitate to prescribe lager beer because its nourishing properties were beneficial to those who required a mild restorative, and it invigorated and nourished the system. During its early years, the brewery employed eleven people and turned out about fifteen thousand barrels of beer annually. A one-half-mile-long spur line was built from the Cheshire Railroad to the brewery, and the company purchased its own locomotive to move freight cars and transport employees.

In addition to the brewery itself, the company built a bottling house, several dwellings and a large boardinghouse. The brewery employed up to sixty or seventy people during peak periods. Five thousand barrels of beer could be stored in the company's Walpole vats.

The name of the company, and presumably the ownership, changed several times. At one time, it was known as Bellows Falls Brewing Company and as Crescent Brewing Company a few years later. Perhaps the best remembered name is Mountain Spring Brewing Company. The brewery had a sales office in Boston, where the beer could be sent quickly by train. The final owners advertised four different beers: Old German Lager, Wurzburger Lager, Canterbury Ale and Golden Cream Ale.

New Hampshire corporate records indicate that the company closed in 1907, almost thirty years after it opened. It probably faced competition from larger breweries and may still have been suffering the lingering financial impact of a serious factory fire on September 7, 1905. The Mountain Spring Brewery, Cheshire County's first large-scale commercial brewery, closed for good well over a century ago.

CHERRY VALLEY

Christopher Robb was born in Fitzwilliam, New Hampshire, in November 1826. The family soon moved to Stoddard, and when Chris was a young man, he joined his father working in his sawmill and pail shop enterprise on Ball Brook.

Chris Robb opened his own mill in 1853, launching a company that would soon become one of the largest and most successful in the history of the town. The product line was expanded from lumber and pails to include clothespins, oil cans, lawnmower handles, baseball bats, rocking chairs, rolling pins, wooden bowls and many other items.

Chris began to purchase abandoned farmland in Stoddard and soon owned approximately ten thousand acres in Stoddard and surrounding towns. He incorporated his firm as the Stoddard Lumber Company in 1884. By that time, the company employed sixty people and did $150,000 worth of business annually.

In addition to several huge mill buildings, the Stoddard Lumber Company owned and operated sixteen farms, a boardinghouse, a general store, a gristmill, a laundry, a blacksmith shop and a wagon shop. The mills, boardinghouse and several other buildings were nestled in a valley along the river. The small village was given the name Cherry Valley because of the cherry trees that grew there. The firm also counted among its assets forty horses, a Concord Coach and a steamboat named for Robb's daughter Myra. Chris Robb was a wealthy, successful businessman when he died from angina at age sixty-seven in 1894.

The headquarters of Christopher Robb's vast logging and woodenware business was located here in Cherry Valley, where water power was readily available.

Chris's son-in-law Charlie Merrill, a former mill hand for the company who had married the boss's daughter, took over the operation of the company. Townspeople say that Merrill lacked the business ability of his father-in-law. The mill complex burned in 1907, and there was no effort to rebuild. Within a few years, a maze of overgrown stone foundations was the only evidence of Chris Robb's woodenware kingdom at Cherry Valley.

TEMPLE LITHIA SPRING

Sidney Scammon opened the Pack Monadnock Lithia Spring in Temple, New Hampshire, during the year 1891. He set up a springhouse and began to sell bottles of the water.

The water was advertised as the most "wonderful Natural Lithia Spring Water known in the world." Because of the high concentration of lithium and other elements, the water was proclaimed to be the best remedy for kidney trouble and indigestion. It was also advertised as therapeutic for rheumatism, eczema, diabetes and Bright's disease.

The park became a popular recreation area for local residents. Scammon built a picnic area, playground, bandstand and ballfield at the spring and invited the public to use the facilities. The spring became famous, and wagonloads of bottled lithia water were hauled to local railroad stations and shipped throughout the country. Scammon and his partner, his uncle Rodney Killam, a lifelong resident of Temple, were looked on as leading citizens of the town.

A 1904 newspaper report indicated that Killam was unusually busy filling orders for the water. For twenty years, the spring was one of Temple's greatest attractions. In 1911, however, someone discovered that Scammon was buying large supplies of lithium on a regular basis. It suddenly became clear that the "wonderful Natural Lithia Spring Water" was not natural after all. Scammon had been mixing it!

When the news of the deception became known, Scammon and Uncle Rodney Killam, now eighty-three years old, were forced to leave town in a hurry. They quickly moved to Malden, Massachusetts. The spring was sold to a local lumber company, the trees in the park were removed and the Pack Monadnock Lithia Spring water company ceased to exist.

CLIPPER MOWERS AND REAPERS

During the 1860s, Keene farmer and businessman James Bixby Elliot purchased stock in the Clipper Mower and Reaper Company of Yonkers, New York. The company made large horse-drawn mowing machines and hay rakes. By the late 1870s, the business was failing, and Elliot moved the firm to Keene in an attempt to salvage the business. Through extensive advertising and a quality product, Elliot built the Clipper Mowing Company into one of Keene's most successful businesses.

The Clipper factory was located at South Keene near the train station there. The firm made several sizes of mowing machines for one or two horses, as well as hay rakes, harrows and potato diggers. The company had its own foundry to forge the metal parts. Clipper machines were advertised as the strongest on the market, with steel fingers and a cast-iron frame. The Clipper mower won thirty-nine first-prize premiums at fairs and shows across the country in 1869.

Elliot built up a successful business with sales agents from Portland, Maine, to San Francisco, California. Clipper machines were sold across the country and throughout Europe.

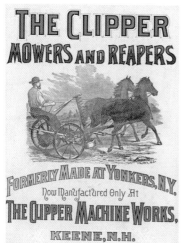

Catalogue of the Clipper Machine Works, manufacturers of award-winning horse-drawn mowers and reapers.

James Elliot passed away in 1888, and the factory, land and fifty finished mowers were sold at auction the following spring for $8,000. The company continued to operate until June 1891, when a spark from a passing locomotive started a fire on the roof. Within one and a half hours, the entire factory was gone.

Young Harry Kingsbury of Keene purchased what parts could be salvaged after the fire and repaired Clipper machines at his Wilkins Toy Company in Keene for several years. The factory was never rebuilt, however, and that was the end of the nationally acclaimed Clipper Mower and Reaper Company.

Shoveling the Way

Charles A. Way was born in Lempster, New Hampshire, in 1836. As a young man, he sailed around Cape Horn to California and took a job in a furniture factory in San Francisco. He returned to New Hampshire and settled in Charlestown in about 1865. He married Caroline White in 1867 and began a family the next year.

Way was an enterprising businessman. He opened a mill in North Charlestown, where he manufactured an unusual and amazing variety of products. The mill turned out chair stock, carriage bows, wooden knitting needles, fishing rods and toy harps.

Way himself was an excellent harpist. He may have learned this skill in California, where he also learned to speak Spanish. The manufacturing census of 1870 indicated that Way produced one hundred velocipedes (early bicycles) from ash and iron during that year. Velocipedes had first been introduced in the region only one year earlier.

There was also one additional product made by Way in North Charlestown. In 1877, he invented a metal clasp that held together the handle and the scoop of a shovel. The result was a practical and reliable snow shovel, which was also produced at the mill in North Charlestown.

Way died in 1908. Few people today have ever heard of him, but snow shovel wielders everywhere owe a debt of gratitude to Charlestown's talented Charles A. Way.

Moving Up with Nathan Ames

Nathan Ames was born in Roxbury, New Hampshire, in November 1825. He was the third child of Daniel and Laura Ames. Nathan attended local schools before the family moved to Saugus, Massachusetts. Young Nathan then attended Phillips Andover Academy and went on to attend Harvard, where he graduated in 1848. He studied law and was admitted to the bar in 1853. During the same year, he released a popular book of poetry.

Ames became a patent attorney, but he also held several patents himself. He invented some ingenious devices during his short life. He invented a machine to improve the polishing of leather at a time when the shoe industry in Lynn, Massachusetts, near his home in Saugus, was one of the largest in the world. In the mid-1850s, he also invented a polygraph. This was an early copying machine that made use of a wire attached to multiple pens. When a person manually used one pen to write on a piece of paper, the wire would move the attached pens on adjacent pieces of paper to create duplicate copies of what was being written. Scientific literature of the day proclaimed that the copying machine made perfect copies with ease.

It is one final invention, however, for which Ames is best remembered today. On March 9, 1859, Nathan Ames patented an invention he called "revolving stairs." The invention was described as a power-driven set of stairs on an endless belt that could ascend or descend continuously. The moving staircase would be used as a means of traveling between floors or levels in subways, buildings and other mass pedestrian areas. Unfortunately, Ames passed away a few years later at age thirty-nine before he had the opportunity to build his new revolving stairs.

It was more than thirty years later that George Wheeler of New York submitted a similar patent. In 1896, he introduced the first working model of his invention and opened it as a novelty ride at New York's Coney Island. Despite Wheeler's success with revolving stairs, Nathan Ames, the farm boy born in Roxbury in 1825, is recognized as the inventor of the escalator.

THE LUMBER KING

George Van Dyke was born in Quebec in 1846. He did not own a pair of shoes until he was eleven years old and attended school for only four years. As a youngster, he left home to find work and took a job as a logger on the Connecticut River. Van Dyke became a river-driver working on the log drives that floated timber down the river each year. He soon became a foreman of the log drives and passed along the western border of Cheshire County many times as his crews worked their logs down the river. Van Dyke probably knew the saloons of North Walpole like the back of his hand.

He soon went into business for himself and opened his own mills. Even after he became a millionaire lumberman and passed his sixtieth birthday, however, he continued to follow the drives down the Connecticut. The drive of 1909 was his biggest ever, containing 53 million feet of timber.

In August of that year, as he walked with the drive through Bellows Falls, Van Dyke sprained his ankle very badly in the riverbed. As a result, he had to follow the drive in his Stanley Steamer auto the next week. At Turners Falls, he and his chauffeur pulled up in the Steamer to watch the drive from an embankment seventy-five feet above the river. No one knows what happened next, whether Van Dyke ordered the chauffeur to drive closer to the edge or the driver made a fatal mistake, but the car plunged over the edge into the river. George Van Dyke died later that day after plunging into the river of which he had been king for so many years.

THE GREATEST MERCHANT IN THE UNITED STATES

John G. Shedd was born in Alstead Center, New Hampshire, in 1850, the youngest of eight children of William and Abigail Shedd. The Shedd family soon moved to Langdon, where John grew up on the family farm. A story is told that while he was gathering sap on the farm one year when he was a teenager, John spilled a bucket of sap, filling his boot with the liquid in the process. He immediately decided that farming would not be his future occupation.

He soon went to work as a clerk at Tufts Store in Alstead's Papermill Village. He later went on to work as a clerk in stores in Bellows Falls and Ludlow, Vermont. In 1872, Shedd moved to Chicago, where he took a job as a stock clerk at the Marshall Field Company, earning twelve dollars a week. He worked his way up in the company, gaining increasing responsibilities as he went.

Shedd returned to New Hampshire in 1878 long enough to marry Mary Porter, the daughter of Dr. Winslow Porter of Alstead. The couple returned to Chicago, where John continued his work at Marshall Field; he became a partner in the firm in 1893 and was appointed vice president eight years later. Marshall Field himself, owner of the rapidly growing firm, described John Shedd as "the greatest merchant in the United States."

John Shedd became president of the company upon the death of Field in 1906. Under Shedd's leadership, Marshall Field & Company became the largest department store in the world, employing twelve thousand Chicago residents and doing $75 million in business annually.

In 1907, Shedd offered to build a public library for his hometown of Alstead. He oversaw the planning for the new facility, which opened in 1910. Shedd paid more than $65,000 for the granite building and its furnishings. He then set up a trust fund to help with library expenses and donated two thousand new books to add to the shelves. The library was given the name Shedd-Porter Memorial Library, in honor of his parents and his wife's parents.

Back in Chicago, Shedd worked with other business leaders to shape his adopted home into a world-class city. Realizing that many of the world's leading cities had aquariums, Shedd decided to build one for Chicago. This

John G. Shedd, millionaire president of Chicago's Marshall Field & Company department store, donated this public library to his hometown of Alstead.

was his way of giving back to the city that had made him a millionaire. He donated $3 million for the project and worked on the early planning but died before the Shedd Aquarium opened in 1930. It is still one of the city's leading attractions.

John G. Shedd, Alstead native and "the greatest merchant in the United States," passed away in Chicago in 1926.

Thayer Portable Houses

In this day of prefab homes, log cabin kits and tiny houses, it is interesting to note that a Keene firm was advertising portable houses more than one hundred years ago. The Springfield Manufacturing Company, makers of the Springfield Portable House, first came to Keene in 1913. By the 1920s, Oscar H. Thayer had become owner and changed the name to the Thayer Portable House Company.

The company, which was located at 171 Winchester Street, manufactured portable and ready-cut buildings of all kinds. Thayer offered bungalows, camps, garages, boathouses, chicken houses, schools and even churches.

This "two room cottage" was one of two dozen portable houses offered in the Thayer Portable House company 1914 catalogue.

Between four hundred and five hundred buildings were made each year at the Thayer Factory. Many of the building styles were named after local features, such as the name Chesterfield given to the bungalow model. The firm employed twenty people and did an annual business in excess of $100,000 during the 1920s.

The portable houses were built in sections and held together with bolts and specially designed clamps. The ready-cut houses came complete in every detail without a single additional piece of lumber or hardware needed. All locks, nails, window screens and even paint were included.

The Thayer Portable House Company disappeared from the city directories in the mid-1940s. Many of the buildings survive in the region. Mr. Thayer's houses would surely be popular in today's market, where many house kits do not include shingles, nails and even floors in some cases.

DINERS THEN AND NOW

The history of American diners began in 1872, when Providence, Rhode Island entrepreneur Walter Scott began serving sandwiches, pies and chicken from a lunch wagon. Twelve years later, Sam Jones of Worcester expanded on Scott's idea by inviting customers inside the wagon, and the true diner was born. A diner is defined as a factory-built restaurant transported to its site intact or in sections, and it has a counter.

The southwestern New Hampshire region still has several classic American diners serving customers today. Keene itself, with one surviving

Proprietor John Judge posed in front of his popular Johnnie's Diner restaurant on Main Street in Keene in the 1930s.

diner, has been the home of at least ten diners since the 1920s. The city's first diner was Edward Dee's Lunch Wagon, which he located at 92 Main Street in 1921. Dee rolled his lunch wagon into an open space alongside Cypress Street and the railroad tracks, enclosed the base to hide the wheels and opened for business.

The popularity of diners increased dramatically during the Depression, partly because of their inexpensive offerings. Several diners opened in Keene during that period. Dee's Lunch Wagon was followed in 1927 by Redfield's Diner on Railroad Street. By 1937, Keene had three diners: Bartlett's Diner on Railroad Street, Liberty Diner on Main Street and Johnnie's Diner, which had replaced Dee's Lunch Wagon at 92 Main Street. During that year, more than one million people ate in diners every day in this country.

The Liberty Diner met a violent end when it was crushed by a tree during the hurricane of 1938. The Keene Diner billed itself as "Keene's Popular Eating Place." Parker's Diner advertised "cheerful service," while Johnnie's encouraged customers to "try our regular 45¢ dinner."

The diner boom was short-lived, however. A long, slow decline began in the 1950s, when fast-food restaurants appeared at the same time that downtowns began to lose traffic and business. Since 1972, Lindy's has been Keene's only diner. These restaurants are now enjoying a revival, however, due in part to nostalgia and in part to the revival of downtowns. This growing appreciation should ensure that classic diners such as Lindy's will be with us for many years to come.

Chapter 3

DOCTORS AND MEDICINE

Silas Cummings, Doctor

Silas Cummings was born in Fitzwilliam, New Hampshire, in October 1803. He worked on his father's farm as a boy and attended local schools. Cummings then went to Dartmouth College, where he graduated from the school's medical department in 1827. He then returned home to Fitzwilliam to begin a medical practice.

Dr. Cummings's account book for the first two years of his practice has survived. It gives detailed insight into the work of a physician in the late 1820s. Dr. Cummings charged twelve cents for an office visit or house call and the same amount for pulling a tooth. He charged one dollar per day for attending a patient full time and two dollars for delivering a baby and all treatment involved with the pregnancy.

Dr. Cummings also sold medicines to his patients, including bitters, laudanum, opium, sedatives, body plasters and a great variety of colored pills. He also used juniper berries, bloodroot, lime water, rosemary, orange peel and licorice in his treatments. Bleeding was a widely used treatment, and Dr. Cummings kept a ready supply of leeches in his office for that purpose.

July 4, 1827, was a typical day for the doctor. On that day, he made one house call, had five office visits, dressed an injured leg and sold his patients a variety of pills, powders, bitters and one dozen leeches. During a ten-month period in 1827 and 1828, Hannah Rockwood made fifty-five office visits and purchased a great quantity of medicine, running up a bill

Dr. Silas Cummings treated his friends and neighbors in the small town of Fitzwilliam for fifty-five years.

of $18.08. She paid her bill with thirty-seven pounds of ham and veal and fifty-six pounds of butter and cheese.

Silas Cummings also served as town postmaster, served in the state legislature and was active in Fitzwilliam's school association and debate club. He is best remembered for his medical practice, however, which was very successful; he served as doctor for the people of Fitzwilliam for fifty-five years until his death in 1882.

Twitchell Ties the Carotid

Amos Twitchell was born in Dublin, New Hampshire, in 1781. He grew up on the family farm there and attended the village school until he went to the New Ipswich Academy to prepare for college. He went on to receive both his MD and an MA from Dartmouth in 1805.

Two years later, Dr. Twitchell was living and practicing in Marlborough, New Hampshire, when he was called upon to attend to a young militia member named John Taggart, who had been wounded in a mock battle at a militia muster. A pistol had been discharged too close to his head, and the discharge of the gun had caused considerable damage to the bone and muscle on the right side of his neck and face. Twitchell found that Taggart's external carotid artery had been damaged but was not bleeding heavily. The external carotid artery supplies blood to the neck and face.

The doctor treated the man for several days, by which time he began to recover. After several more days of treatment and healing, there was only a small wound of two or three inches in diameter. The carotid artery lay at the bottom of the wound, and Dr. Twitchell feared that it might rupture. He warned the young man's mother of this possibility when he visited the house one day. As Twitchell was leaving the yard that day, the mother yelled that her son was bleeding badly.

Twitchell returned to the house and found that the artery had ruptured; blood was spurting three to four feet in the air. He stopped the flow by using his left hand to hold the artery against the base of the skull. The doctor then removed the damaged portion of the artery and was able to suture the blood vessel. It leaked a bit thereafter, but Twitchell packed the wound with a sponge. When the packing was removed a few days later, the artery had healed. The wound itself healed, and Taggart eventually recovered.

Twitchell was not performing a procedure that he had read about in a textbook or learned about in class, because only two other doctors had performed this surgery successfully a short time before, and neither one had published their methods. The young doctor had successfully performed a delicate and difficult new procedure with the help of only the poor man's mother. Three years later, Dr. Twitchell moved to Keene, where he practiced and lived the rest of his life. He became one of the state's leading physicians, pioneering or improving upon numerous medical procedures.

LESURE'S VETERINARY MEDICINES

John G. Lesure of Keene has been credited with having begun the first line of veterinary medicines in the country. Lesure was born in Barnard, Vermont, in the 1840s and began his work with horses as a blacksmith in Royalton. He branched out into the livery business, which he pursued for several years.

As he worked with horses, Lesure tried to find ways to cure their ailments. He became so experienced at this that his neighbors began to bring their horses to him. At that point, he decided to study under a trained veterinarian and was soon devoting all his time to equine diseases and their treatment.

Lesure's medicines became so popular that he opened J.G. Lesure & Co. in Keene in 1885 to manufacture the medicines. The medicines were developed in the company laboratory at 144 Winchester Street. Other companies soon imitated Lesure's group of medicines, but he continued to have the largest line in the country. In the 1890s, he had three traveling salesmen and shipped his products to stores across the United States.

Among Lesure' s many remedies were the All Healing Balm, Electric Hoof Ointment, Worm Annihilator, Veterinary Fever Drops and Lesure's

John G. Lesure delivered his line of veterinarian medicines in this decorated delivery wagon.

Veterinary Colic Cure. John G. Lesure operated the business for sixteen years until his death in 1901. His family continued Lesure's Veterinary Medicines into the 1930s.

Dr. Twitchell and the Farmer

Dr. Amos Twitchell of Keene lectured and wrote about the danger of tobacco use during the early years of the nineteenth century, long before it was confirmed that tobacco caused serious health problems. A story about Dr. Twitchell and one of his patients illustrates his views on tobacco use.

One day in his travels, Dr. Twitchell met a farmer from whom he often purchased grain. The farmer looked miserable, and Dr. Twitchell asked about the man's health. The farmer replied, "Almost gone, doctor. I shall never bring you any more corn. The physicians have all given up and tell

Dr. Amos Twitchell was one of New Hampshire's most skilled and renowned physicians of the nineteenth century.

me I am dying of consumption." Dr. Twitchell said that he was sorry that he would get no more corn but that he thought he might be able to cure the man. The farmer replied that it was too late and that he must prepare to die.

The doctor offered to make a bargain with the man. The farmer had to agree to follow Twitchell's prescription for three months. If he recovered, he was to pay the doctor fifty bushels of corn, but if he died, the doctor would pay the man's family the equivalent of the corn in cash. After some hesitation, the man agreed. Dr. Twitchell directed the man to take the tobacco from his mouth and never to touch tobacco again in any form.

Six months later, the doctor met up with the man, who was apparently in perfect health, and claimed the corn. The man refused, saying that his wife thought fifty bushels of corn was more than his life was worth. The two compromised, and the farmer gave Dr. Twitchell three or four bushels of corn and a bushel of white beans.

THE BRATTLEBORO WATER CURE

During the mid-1800s, Brattleboro was the home of the nation's most famous water cure institution. Water cures involved hydropathic physical therapy, including ice cold baths and plunges, and strictly prescribed diets and exercise programs.

The Brattleboro water cure was established by Dr. Robert Wesselhoeft in the mid-1840s. By 1846, there were 392 patients, overflowing the cure building and local hotels, so that patients had to board with local residents. The business was such a success that a competitor, the Lawrence water cure, was opened across the street in 1853. Patients at the Wesselhoeft cure were required to bathe in water of a specific temperature for a specified length of time each day.

Strict diets were prescribed; coffee, tea and warm bread were forbidden. Patients were never to read or write after supper and had to retire at 10:00 p.m. each evening. The treatment was not billed as a cure-all, but patients were guaranteed a speedy and radical cure to their ailments if they followed their treatment exactly as prescribed.

Many felt that the water cure was a new fake get-rich-quick scheme. The *Boston Medical and Surgical Journal* and several local newspapers gave unfavorable reviews or ridiculed the cure.

Despite this, the Brattleboro cure was very popular. Harriet Beecher Stowe, Henry Wadsworth Longfellow, Martin Van Buren, General William Tecumseh Sherman, General George B. McClellan and many other famous patients came here for treatment. They did much more than take cold plunges, however. The patients also hiked in the woods, picnicked on the riverbank, played outdoor games and attended elegant balls and dances.

The cost of the treatment was ten dollars per week. During and after the Civil War, the water cure lost its important southern clientele, and the buildings were soon converted to summer hotels.

Chapter 4

TRAVEL AND
TRANSPORTATION

VILLAGE BRIDGE IN WALPOLE

The Village Bridge in Walpole was a covered bridge that spanned the Connecticut River and connected Walpole with Westminster, Vermont. The bridge was opened to the public in the fall of 1870 with a grand celebration. A wooden toll bridge had preceded the Village Bridge at that location. Two floods, in 1867 and 1868, caused serious damage, first to the west end and then to the east end of the bridge. The owners of the toll bridge turned the structure over to the Towns of Walpole and Westminster, and a new free bridge was constructed across the river.

The new covered bridge served travelers for forty years after the opening celebration in 1870. On April 1, 1910, a fire on the bridge was reported at 8:15 p.m. The volunteer firefighters responded immediately, but the structure was fully engulfed in flames when they arrived. The spectacular blaze destroyed the bridge.

Arson was suspected, and an investigation was begun. George Tiffany reported that he had seen Arthur Norrington on the bridge just before the blaze broke out. Shortly thereafter, Norrington, a resident of Westminster, confessed to the crime. His wife had a job with the Holland family in Walpole, and it seems that Norrington's motive in setting the fire was to prevent her from crossing the bridge to go to work. He did not want his wife to work in Walpole and felt that she would have to stay at home in Westminster if the bridge was gone.

The Village Bridge carried traffic across the Connecticut River for forty years before it was destroyed by fire in 1910.

Norrington accomplished his purpose, for a while at least, but the authorities did not care for his methods. He was sent to the state prison, where he died three years later. Westminster and Walpole were soon linked again, as a new bridge was built within a year or two to replace Walpole's old Village Bridge.

THE FATE OF THE BRITTON FERRY

Ferries were once common on the Connecticut River, carrying passengers, wagons and produce from shore to shore. Throughout the nineteenth century, however, more and more bridges were built across the river, and the ferries began to disappear. Several ferries operated well into the twentieth century, however. The Britton Ferry in Westmoreland survived until it met a disastrous fate during the early years of automobile travel.

On a late summer day in 1930, the 5:00 p.m. ferry left Putney and started for the Westmoreland landing. Two automobiles, six passengers and Mr. Cushing, the ferry operator, were on board. Harry Pierce, one of the

The Britton Ferry transported passengers and vehicles from Westmoreland to Putney, Vermont, on the opposite shore of the Connecticut River.

passengers, noticed water pouring into the right front corner of the boat. He alerted Mr. Cushing, who asked Pierce to back his car up a little.

Water continued to enter the boat, however, and Ray Austin, the owner of the second auto, was also instructed to back up a bit. He backed too far, however, and struck the apron of the boat. The ferry immediately filled with water and sank. Pierce, Cushing and another passenger, Thomas Carpenter, swam toward the New Hampshire shore. They reached the landing safely with the assistance of some people who were on the shore at the time.

Ray Austin, his wife, his daughter and William Clark, another passenger in the Austin vehicle, could not escape from their car before the ferry sank. All four of them drowned; their bodies were all recovered from the river by the following morning.

The ferry was salvaged but was condemned and never ran again. This 1930 accident brought a sad end to more than 175 years of Westmoreland ferry service.

RUNAWAY TRAIN

Many local residents realize that downtown Keene is located on an ancient glacial lakebed. As a result, most of the city is surrounded by hills. This proved to be a problem when the railroad proposed a line through Keene in the 1840s because the locomotives could not pull heavy freight cars up steep hills. The Cheshire Railroad engineers and construction crews were up to the task, but it was not easy. They had to cut through granite ledges, remove the tops from hills and add many tons of fill to keep the grade manageable to get trains in and out of the city.

The railroad placed an extra locomotive and engineer in Westmoreland to help push trains coming from Walpole up and over the height of land at the Summit cut before they started down into the city. The Summit, along what is now Route 12 near the border of Westmoreland and Surry, was six hundred feet in elevation above Cold River station in Walpole, making this one of the steepest stretches of railroad in New England. Extra locomotives also had to go out from the Keene station to help push heavy trains out of the city and over the Summit as they headed north.

Around 1900, the railroad itself inadvertently produced a clear illustration of Keene's location in a bowl at the bottom of a valley. One morning, a long freight train left the station on Main Street and headed toward Walpole. The locomotive slowly made its way up and over the Summit without help from another locomotive. This may have been accomplished because unknown to the engineer, the last couple of cars and the caboose became detached near the top of the hill. A few moments passed before they began slowly moving in the wrong direction.

The heavy cars quickly gained speed as they hurtled back into the city and toward Keene's busy Main Street crossing. The flagman on Main Street saw the train cars coming just in time to rush out and stop traffic before they sped across Main Street. The cars continued on and disappeared from sight. Near the Webb Station in Marlborough, as the freight moved up the hills on the south side of the city, they finally came to a stop, but only for a second, before they began to roll back toward Keene once again.

Once again, the cars hurtled across Main Street and headed for the Summit. Near the top of the hill, they began their return trip. This continued for some time, with the train moving too fast at Main Street for anyone to jump on and apply the brakes. Gravity and friction finally slowed the train enough for a brakeman to jump aboard as the cars moved through the railyards yet again. He was able to stop the freight cars and caboose.

The old-timers who gathered on Main Street regularly had caught wind of the excitement and gathered at the station to watch the cars seesawing through downtown. They even placed bets on the time of the next arrival. They were surely disappointed when the runaway train show came to an end.

KEENE ELECTRIC RAILWAY

Most residents of our region realize the economic importance of the railroad to the history of Keene. The city was also the home of a trolley system, however, during the first quarter of the twentieth century. The idea of building a street railway system in Keene was introduced in 1887, when a company was chartered to build such a line. This was a time when trolley building was taking place across the country. Other lines were proposed in the county, but the Keene line was the only one to be built.

The Keene Electric Railway Company did not actually begin to carry passengers until September 10, 1900. At 6:15 a.m., the first car left Central Square in Keene on its way to Marlborough village. The company owned and operated eight and a half miles of track. From Central Square, the tracks ran in three directions: out West Street to Wheelock Park, south to Wilson Pond in Swanzey and east to Marlborough village. The trolley was an important element of Keene life for the next twenty-five years.

The company purchased land in Swanzey and created the Wilson Pond Recreation Area. A dance hall, theater, boxing matches, swimming in the

A Keene Electric Railway trolley car, demonstrating a fender designed to protect the car from obstructions on the tracks.

pond and other activities resulted in a ready clientele for the trolley. Fifteen million passengers rode the trolley line during its history, but the company was never a moneymaker.

It was the introduction of motorized buses, however, that finally brought the trolley to an end. The company purchased six buses in May 1926, but the trolley cars continued to operate through the Fourth of July holiday. The next morning, a full bus operation began, and the Keene Electric Railway passed from the scene forever.

CRASH AT THE DRIVING PARK

The safety of air travel has been of primary concern across the country and around the world since the early days of the twentieth century. In the Keene vicinity, there have been relatively few air disasters. Airplane crashes were not entirely unknown here in the early days of aviation, however. A 1911 plane crash at the Keene Driving Park, now the location of the Edgewood neighborhood, was the first in Keene.

Professor Bonnette's airplane at the Keene Driving Park before it took off from the racecourse and promptly crashed into a tree.

On the Fourth of July that year, a large crowd gathered at the Driving Park to enjoy a day of parades, concerts, baseball, fireworks and the first airplane flight originating from Keene. This was just a few years after the Wright brothers made the first successful airplane flight at Kitty Hawk.

The crowd in Keene that day came to see the flying machine of Professor Clarence Bonnette of Vermont. Bonnette was a longtime balloonist who had built his first airplane the previous year. His plane was a Curtiss-type frame apparatus similar to the one built by the Wright brothers. The pilot sat within the metal framework, and the plane rested on three bicycle wheels. The engine was behind the pilot, and a seven-foot propeller was attached to the rear of the engine. The combined weight of the airplane and pilot was six hundred pounds.

On the allotted day and time, Bonnette piloted his small plane down the driving track and lifted off into the air. Local reports indicate that the machine continued some distance and rose fifteen or twenty feet in the air before striking a tree and promptly crashing back to earth. Professor Bonnette was not injured, but the same could not be said for the airplane.

The large crowd that gathered at the driving park on that Fourth of July was not impressed with the demonstration. Their dissatisfaction was a topic of discussion in the *Keene Sentinel* newspaper for some time thereafter. This first flight was not a success, but it did not deter aviation buffs in Keene. The city was a leader in aviation in the state, and the Keene Airport opened in the autumn of 1928.

WALPOLE BARNSTORMER

Harry Bingham Brown was born in Walpole, New Hampshire, in 1883. He grew up on the family farm and attended local schools. By 1910, he had moved to Boston and entered the grocery business.

It was around this time that Harry became involved in aviation as an early pilot. It is not known where this Walpole farm boy learned to fly, but he became one of the leading barnstormers in the early days of aviation. Barnstormers were pilots who traveled around the country performing stunts and selling airplane rides. This was a time when airplanes were little more than tubes, wires, braces and an engine, all of which were out in the open.

In 1911 and 1912, Brown did experimental work in Washington. He demonstrated the possible military use of airplanes by taking a National Guard member up to make observations and illustrated how messages could be dropped from the aircraft using small parachutes. He also carried a rifleman into the air to illustrate that marksmen could be accurate shooting from airplanes. Brown's personal plane was a Wright biplane.

In 1912, he took passenger Isabel Patterson into the air at the Aeronautical Society meet at Staten Island. Brown and his passenger soon rose to the height of 5,300 feet, breaking the American altitude record for an airplane. It was also in 1912 that Brown made the first fly-over of the city of Keene. There were no airfields in the city then, so the flight probably originated from his parents' farm in Walpole.

Brown became acquainted with pioneer balloonist and aviation promoter Leo Stevens. Stevens became manager for Harry Brown and a parachute jumper named Lapham, sending them around the country and beyond. Brown offered rides and performed stunts, and Lapham leaped from Brown's biplane. On New Year's Day 1913, Brown flew for fifty-eight minutes over New York.

The barnstormer almost lost his life when he and Lapham performed in Puerto Rico in 1913. His plane rapidly toppled hundreds of feet toward the ocean that day. Brown saw a large group of sharks feeding below him and feared that they would soon be feeding on him, but the plane leveled off two hundred feet before it reached the water, and he managed to land safely.

Harry Brown toured the United States, the West Indies and the eastern provinces of Quebec for four years. He also did some flying in the 1914 movie *The Perils of Pauline*. Interestingly, he married a woman named Pauline later that year. In October 1914, Brown married Pauline McLeod in Boston. Pauline was surely aware of his near miss in Puerto Rico and asked him to stop flying. He agreed, and the couple resumed a quiet life in Jamaica Plain, Massachusetts, where he became a plumber. Some years later, the couple returned to Harry's hometown of Walpole, where he took up his father's profession of farming. He passed away there in 1954 and is buried in the Village Cemetery.

Plumbing and farming were certainly less exciting than performing aerial stunts, but Walpole's Harry Bingham Brown had experienced four years of excitement as a star barnstormer during the early years of American aviation history.

The Old Arch Bridge

The steel arch bridge that spanned the Connecticut River between North Walpole and Bellows Falls was built during 1904 and 1905. During the

The second-longest highway arch bridge in the United States opened in 1905, connecting the villages of North Walpole, New Hampshire, and Bellows Falls, Vermont.

previous years, the population of the two villages had increased rapidly, and the old Tucker Toll Bridge was insufficient for the increased traffic.

The new structure, built by Shoemaker & Company of Philadelphia at a cost of almost $45,000, was the second-longest highway arch in the United States and the longest with the roadway itself suspended from the arch. The span was nearly 650 feet in length.

The new arch was opened on March 20, 1905, with a grand celebration. The local band played on the bridge and later at Russell Memorial Hall, where the formal celebration was held. Church bells were rung in both villages, and fireworks were displayed.

The bridge was opened to traffic and did its job for almost seventy years. It survived the flood of 1927, when the roadway at the east end was completely washed away, along with houses on the riverbank. In 1971, the bridge was declared unsafe and closed to traffic. It was said to be unsafe even for foot traffic.

The National Trust for Historic Preservation fought a losing battle to renovate and save the historic bridge. It was decided to build a new $5 million bridge and remove the 1905 arch. The demolition was to occur late in 1982. Explosives were set in place early in December. When the smoke cleared, however, the bridge still stood, and crowds along the riverbank cheered.

Three more blasts were attempted, but the bridge, which had been declared unsafe ten years earlier, still stood. Finally, torches were used to cut the steel supports, and the historic arch bridge fell quietly into the river and disappeared under the water.

Chapter 5

FAME AND FORTUNE

CHENEY'S EXPRESS SUCCESS

Benjamin Pierce Cheney was born in Hillsborough, New Hampshire, in August 1815. He was the oldest child of Jesse and Alice Cheney. At the age of ten, young Cheney left school to go to work in his father's blacksmith shop. Two years later, he went to work at a tavern in Francestown, New Hampshire.

It was at the age of sixteen, however, that he began a job that was to change his life. Cheney took a job as a stagecoach driver. For six years, he drove the fifty-mile stage route from Keene to Nashua one day and the return route back again the next day. On one of his long daily runs, he met Daniel Webster, with whom he formed a lifelong friendship.

In 1842, the young stage driver established Cheney and Company's Express, which ran from Boston to Montreal. Freight was carried by train from Boston to Concord, New Hampshire, and then by stage to Montreal. Ten years after starting his business, Cheney began to buy out his competitors.

He soon formed the United States and Canada Express Company, serving all of northern New England. In 1879, Cheney's large express company was merged with the American Express Company. Cheney became the largest stockholder of American Express and the company's treasurer.

Benjamin Cheney had become very wealthy. He held interest in the Wells Fargo Company and was an early promoter of the Northern Pacific Railroad.

He and his family built a beautiful estate in Wellesley, Massachusetts, which extended for one mile along the Charles River.

Cheney became a well-known philanthropist, donating money to many causes. He donated $50,000 to Dartmouth College and gave funds for the formation of Cheney Academy in Washington State. Perhaps Benjamin Cheney's most well-known donation was that of a bronze statue that stands in front of the State House in Concord. The statue is of native son Daniel Webster, the passenger who became Cheney's friend on the long stage ride many years earlier.

SCIENTIST JOHN LOCKE

John Locke was born in February 1792 in the town of Lempster. His father, Samuel Locke, was a farmer and millwright in that community. Young John attended classes at Yale, studied medicine with a Keene doctor from 1816 to 1818 and graduated in 1819 from the Yale medical department. He then went on to serve as curator of Harvard's Botanical Garden, as a navy surgeon and as a teacher at a girls' seminary in Vermont.

Locke then moved south and opened Locke's Female Seminary in Lexington, Kentucky. He moved the Female Seminary to Cincinnati in the 1830s. Although he lived in Cincinnati the rest of his life, Locke traveled as the geologist with exploration parties in the Northwest Territories. He became a professor of chemistry and pharmacy at Ohio Medical College in 1836, a position that he held for many years.

This man of many talents is recognized as a pioneer in the fields of botany, geology and electricity. He invented many instruments for use in optics, physics, electricity and magnetism. Among these was the electro-chronograph, which was purchased by the United States government and used to improve the accuracy of longitude determinations. In his spare time, Locke wrote textbooks on botany and English grammar. Lempster native and leading scientist John Locke passed away in Cincinnati in July 1856.

THE LABORS OF CARROLL WRIGHT

Carroll D. Wright was born in Dunbarton in 1840. His family moved to Washington, New Hampshire, when he was three years old. He attended the local elementary school there. His teacher was Miss Sarah Shedd. She had been one of the original New England mill girls, traveling from her home in Washington to work in the textile mills in Lowell, Massachusetts. When she returned to teach at Washington, she often told her students of her working experiences and discussed labor and economic history. These discussions had a profound impact on young Carroll Wright.

He later attended local academies and went on to study law in Keene in 1860. He interrupted his studies to serve in the Civil War, rising from private to the rank of colonel of the Fourteenth New Hampshire Regiment. After the war, he returned to Keene, where he was admitted to the bar in 1865.

Two years later, he left Keene and began to practice law in Boston. He soon became involved in politics and was appointed supervisor of the census for Massachusetts in 1880. Wright became a lecturer on labor and the economy and had soon published dozens of volumes on those topics.

Because of the interest fostered by his former elementary school teacher, Wright became one of the foremost labor and economy scholars in the nation. In 1885, former Washington schoolboy and Keene lawyer Carroll D. Wright was appointed as the first commissioner of labor for the United States of America, a post that he held for the next seventeen years.

ON THE WINGS OF AN ANGEL

Larkin G. Mead was born in Chesterfield, New Hampshire, in January 1835. The Mead family moved across the river to Brattleboro when young Larkin was four years old. As a boy, he displayed a taste for art and was constantly drawing and sculpting.

After studying under a sculptor in New York for a short time in the 1850s, Mead returned to Brattleboro and began to teach drawing at the old town hall. Late in 1856, he conceived an idea for a bit of fun to bring in the New Year. On New Year's Eve, three days before his twenty-second birthday, Larkin Mead sculpted an angel of snow in downtown Brattleboro.

With two friends as assistants, he worked late into the night sculpting his angel alongside North Main Street. Mead inspected the sculpture by lantern light when he was finished and, satisfied with his work, went home to bed. Little did he realize that this "snow angel" was about to change his life!

The next day, the residents of Brattleboro were astounded by the remarkable beauty of this sculpture of snow. Word of the snow angel spread, and crowds gathered to view the work. The story of the angel was recorded in local newspapers and eventually in New York papers. The story spread across the country and as far away as Spain. Shortly thereafter, Nicholas Longworth of Cincinnati commissioned Mead to sculpt his snow angel in Vermont marble. Many other commissions soon followed, and Mead was on his way to fame.

Among his more famous works are the sculptures *Agriculture* and *Ethan Allen*, which adorn the Vermont State House, and a series of six sculptures on the Lincoln Monument in Springfield, Illinois. Larkin G. Mead, Chesterfield native, became one of the best-known sculptors of his day after creating his angel of snow on Brattleboro's North Main Street.

The Cheshire Place

Jones Wilder came to Rindge, New Hampshire, in the 1880s. He purchased 7,200 acres there and quickly built up one of the largest farmsteads ever developed in New England.

Wilder had made a fortune in New York as a partner in the Butterick Dress Pattern Company. Many years earlier, as a young man in his twenties, Wilder had failed miserably as a sawmill operator in Rindge, but he returned to the town to build his utopian farm community. Some people felt that he returned to the site of his earlier failure to prove to the townspeople that he was now a success.

Wilder's 7,200 acres included twenty small farms that were all renovated and restocked. He kept a workforce of three hundred to five hundred men busy for the next thirteen years. In addition to the farms, the community included saw-, grist- and cider mills; bobbin and vinegar factories; blacksmith and wheelwright shops; a greenhouse; an animal hospital; a brickyard; tenements; Wilder's mansion; and several windmills that powered an underground water system. The cost of construction was an astounding $800,000.

The farm estate grew, and Wilder opened it to the public in 1893. The Cheshire Improvement Company, also known as the Cheshire Place, was visited by many people who came to study Wilder's farming methods. One year later, however, Wilder died, and the operation of the estate was discontinued. The Butterick Company soon reopened the Cheshire Place on a smaller scale. Much of the estate was sold off during the early years of the 1900s.

During 1926, Wilder's son George purchased the remainder of the property and dismantled most of the original buildings, leaving the mansion intact. George's widow sold the estate upon his death in 1931. Several years later, the remains of Jones Wilder's dream—a few buildings surrounded by cellar holes and endless stone walls—became the home of the Hampshire Country School, which still occupies the site today.

JUBILEE JIM FISK

The name of Jim Fisk is well known to students of United States history as one of the most notorious robber barons of the Victorian era. Fisk was born in Vermont in 1835 and spent his boyhood years in Brattleboro. His father, James Sr., was an itinerant peddler who prospered and built the Revere House hotel in Brattleboro in 1849.

By that time, young Jim Jr. had already spent three years with a traveling circus but returned to Brattleboro to help his father with the hotel. Brattleboro was not exciting enough for young Jim, however, and he soon ventured to other locales. His first adventure in finance occurred during the Civil War, when he speculated in blockaded Southern cotton and the sale of worthless Confederate bonds in England.

After the war, Jim Fisk went to Wall Street and joined in business with Jay Gould. Fisk, Gould and partner Daniel Drew masterminded the takeover of the Erie Railroad and then milked the broken-down line for millions. Perhaps Fisk's greatest exploit was his attempt, with Gould, to corner the gold market. They nearly succeeded in their attempt; the result was the ruin of many investors during the Black Friday panic of September 24, 1869.

Fisk was a very visible public figure who became known as "Jubilee Jim." He was known not only for his financial ability but also for his appetite for expensive things. He loved diamonds and had an enormous capacity for champagne and oysters. It was a woman that resulted in Fisk's untimely demise. Although he was married, it was another woman, Josie Mansfield, who was the great love of his life. Josie herself was involved with yet another man, Ed Stokes, at the same time.

On January 7, 1872, Stokes shot and killed Fisk on the staircase of the Broadway Central Hotel in New York City. Jubilee Jim's massive remains were sent to Brattleboro and lay in state at the Revere House prior to his burial in the Prospect Hill Cemetery. Famous American sculptor and local native Larkin G. Mead created an appropriately large and ornate monument, complete with a bust of Jubilee Jim, to stand on the grave of Brattleboro robber baron Jim Fisk.

The Witch of Wall Street

Henrietta Howland Robinson, known as Hetty, was born in New Bedford, Massachusetts, in 1834. Her father and grandfather were wealthy owners of a New Bedford whaling fleet. Although her family was wealthy, they were frugal. By the age of six, she was reading financial newspapers to her grandfather each day. She became familiar with the world of finance and made her first investment when she opened a bank account at the age of eight.

Hetty inherited several million dollars at age twenty-one and began to use the funds on Wall Street. She met Edward Henry Green when she was in her early thirties. Edward was tall, handsome and already wealthy. He agreed to a prenuptial agreement foregoing all rights to her money, and the couple was married in 1867. They had two children, Ned and Sylvia.

Hetty invested in real estate, mortgages and railroads, and her fortune increased dramatically. Edward purchased his grandfather's old house in Bellows Falls in 1879 and moved his family to Vermont. Unfortunately, Edward went bankrupt in 1885, and he and Hetty separated when she refused to pay his debts. Hetty returned to New York, where she became a legend as the richest woman in America—and a miser.

Hetty was a shrewd investor at a time when this field was limited almost exclusively to men. Despite her wealth, however, she never spent more than she needed to survive. It is said that she never turned on the heat in her house or used hot water. She wore only one dress until it became worn out, and then she bought another. One story suggests that she searched for hours for a lost two-cent stamp. Another tale recounts that she refused to pay a doctor to treat her son's injured leg, resulting in amputation.

One day, Hetty and her children arrived at the Keene railroad station on the 9:23 a.m. train from Bellows Falls on their way to Dublin, New Hampshire. The ticket agent offered to arrange for a carriage to drive them to Dublin, but she declined to pay for a carriage. Instead, Hetty, Ned and Sylvia sat in the station for several hours waiting for the afternoon train to Harrisville. Many townspeople made their way to the station when they learned that the richest woman in the country was there in the waiting room.

Hetty and Edward reconciled toward the end of his life, and she returned to Bellows Falls to care for him. After his death, she always wore a heavy black dress as she walked along Wall Street. This was probably the origin of her nickname, the "Witch of Wall Street."

Hetty was not affected by her miserly reputation. She walked to the grocery store in Bellows Falls, where she bought broken cookies because they were cheaper and returned her berry boxes for a nickel refund. Hetty Green died in 1916 and was buried with her husband in Bellows Falls. Her estate of over $100 million would be worth more than $2 billion today.

VAUDEVILLE PIONEER

Benjamin Franklin Keith was born in Hillsborough, New Hampshire, in 1846. Keith was so thrilled by the traveling circuses of his childhood that he moved to New York as a young man to work for the circus. After working for several shows, he decided to open his own.

In 1883, he rented a dime museum, a collection of stationary exhibits of curiosities, in Boston. Keith added a live premature baby, a chicken with a human face and a pair of comedians to his show. He then transformed his lobby into a Japanese garden and hired a troupe of singers. This was the first continuous performance show in America.

This first vaudeville show was a huge success, and vaudeville spread throughout the country. Keith soon did away with the animal exhibits and worked hard to refine the entertainment at his Gaiety Theatre. He brought in legitimate stage stars and offered them handsome salaries to work with his show.

Keith used his new riches to build a truly lavish new theater on Washington Street in Boston in 1894. His new theater offered extravagant architecture with stained glass, elaborate ironwork and elegant marble throughout. Most importantly, Keith's two-thousand-seat theater brought in huge profits with thirty performances a week at fifty cents a seat.

He soon opened new show halls across the country. He was also a pioneer in the motion picture business, introducing this new form of entertainment into his vaudeville theaters. Benjamin Franklin Keith, the father of vaudeville, passed away in 1914; by that time, this Hillsborough native was the millionaire owner of four hundred theaters across the United States.

MARK TWAIN IN DUBLIN

Henry D. Allison, storekeeper and postmaster in Dublin, New Hampshire, during the early 1900s, also served as the local real estate agent during Dublin's peak years as a summer resort for the rich and famous. In March 1905, Allison received a message from Mrs. Abbott Thayer indicating that a

The village of Dublin around the time Mark Twain spent two summers writing in the town.

friend of hers was considering coming to Dublin for the summer, if a suitable house could be found. That friend was Samuel Langhorne Clemens, better known by his penname, Mark Twain. Allison found a suitable house, and the Clemens family arrived in May to spend the summer in Dublin. They also returned the next summer (1906) for a second season.

Mark Twain found his summer visits to Dublin both productive and enjoyable. He told a reporter during his first season in Dublin, "It is claimed that the atmosphere of the New Hampshire highlands is exceptionally bracing and stimulating, and a fine aid to hard and continuous work. It is a just claim, I think. I came in May and wrote 35 successive days without a break. It is possible that I could not have done it elsewhere." Twain reportedly worked on his autobiography while summering in Dublin.

Although Twain wrote copiously, he also became involved in social functions and presented lectures while in Dublin. He recited a thrilling tale in the vestry of a church one evening at a sewing circle supper. Orvis Fairbanks was in attendance. Fairbanks worked in the grocery store in Dublin. Henry Allison later wrote that Fairbanks listened with rapt attention to Twain's story, sitting tensely on the edge of his seat. After a half hour, the story came to a sudden climax with a quick, loud shout from

Twain. Fairbanks was so startled that he lost his balance, fell off his seat and landed on the floor. Orvis K. Fairbanks later established the successful O.K. Fairbanks grocery store in Keene.

Twain praised the solitude and beauty of Dublin. He told a reporter, "Dublin is the one place I have always longed for, but never knew existed in fact until now."

MAY YOHE AND THE BLUE DIAMOND INN

May Yohe, known as "Madcap May," was the talk of the theater world in the last decade of the nineteenth century. Born in Bethlehem, Pennsylvania, in 1866, May debuted on stage in a comic opera in Philadelphia in 1886. She quickly made a name for herself, performing in one play after another in New York, Chicago and London.

May played the title character in the hit show *Little Christopher Columbus* in 1894. She was outspoken, daring, confident—and now she was successful. She became a favorite of the Prince of Wales while in England, and in 1894, she married Lord Francis Hope, the possessor of a large fortune and an English estate. May found countless ways to spend Francis's money and enjoy his family treasures, including the famous forty-five-karat Hope Diamond, also known as the Blue Diamond. She apparently did not worry about the supposed curse of the Hope Diamond, which indicated that anyone who possessed the gem would suffer tragedy and heartbreak.

Misfortune began soon enough for the couple, however. They spent Francis's fortune, borrowed money and headed out on a world tour in 1900. While on the tour, they met Bradlee Strong, a captain in the United States Army. May quickly fell in love with Strong and refused to return to England with Francis. May and Francis were divorced, and she quickly married her new love. Her second marriage was even less successful than her first, and May and Bradlee Strong divorced in 1905. There were rumors of other relationships and marriages for May in the next few years. She also returned to the stage on occasion, often with limited success.

By 1910, May was managing a run-down boardinghouse in Seattle. In about 1914, she married yet another military officer, British army captain John Smuts. It was during this marriage that May made her way to Cheshire County. In 1921, May helped write and promote a movie serial titled *The Hope Diamond Mystery*, which starred Boris Karloff. May and John toured the vaudeville circuit with a performance based on the movie. The couple bought and lost a California ranch before spending the remainder of their savings on a farm in Marlow, New Hampshire.

In 1923, May and John opened the Blue Diamond Inn on their property there. They offered meals to the many tourists and other travelers on the Dartmouth College Highway in Marlow. John did the cooking, and May served as hostess and manager. May's management of the inn was publicized in statewide publications, and visitors came to see the former stage star. Misfortune continued to follow her, however, as the inn burned in November 1924. Arson was suspected.

May and John moved to Boston following this most recent loss, where John took a job as a janitor. May died of heart and kidney disease in 1938. Three thousand people attended her funeral. A cellar hole in Marlow is all that remains of the Blue Diamond Inn, but the story of May Yohe lives on, and the infamous Hope Diamond is now on exhibit in the Smithsonian Museum of Natural History.

MR. MARATHON

The spring of 2020 marked the ninetieth anniversary of Clarence DeMar's final victory in the Boston Marathon. DeMar lived in Keene throughout the 1930s while working as a faculty member at Keene Teachers College.

Clarence DeMar began running as a youngster in Ohio. He ran a mile to and from school each day. His family settled in Melrose, Massachusetts, in 1909. The following year, he ran in the Boston Marathon for the first time and finished second. A few months after the race, DeMar's doctor told him he had a heart murmur and he should not be walking up stairs.

Despite this diagnosis and his doctor's advice, he signed up for the Boston Marathon again the following year, in the spring of 1911. The race doctors also told him he had a heart murmur, that he should drop out of the race if he began to feel fatigued and that he should stop running races. Two hours, twenty-one minutes and thirty-nine seconds later, he won the marathon, breaking the Boston time record in the process.

DeMar received a great deal of publicity for the victory, but he was just beginning. He went on to win the marathon in 1922, 1923, 1924, 1927 and 1928. DeMar was already known as "Mr. Marathon" when he moved to Keene in 1929. He taught industrial education and coached the track teams at the college. He wrote in his autobiography that he ran back and forth between Keene and Boston each week, although he would sometimes walk or hitchhike.

Clarence DeMar, known as "Mr. Marathon" (*left*), received an award from the people of Keene, probably soon after winning the Boston Marathon for the seventh time.

DeMar brought honor to the school and the city with his seventh and final victory at Boston in 1930 at the age of forty-one. He ran the Boston Marathon a total of thirty-four times and finished in the top ten fifteen times. He also won marathons at Philadelphia; Providence; Cleveland; Port Chester, New York; and Manchester, New Hampshire. Finally, DeMar ran for the United States Olympic marathon teams in 1912, 1924 and 1928, winning a bronze medal in 1924.

Clarence DeMar's total of seven wins at Boston is more than any other person in the open division. He is still remembered and respected by runners today, more than ninety years after his final Boston victory and more than sixty years after his death. Perhaps he is most fondly remembered in his 1930s home of Keene, where the local Clarence DeMar Marathon has been run in his honor for four decades.

JUNE VINCENT

The Willis Smith family moved to Keene in 1931, when the Reverend Smith became pastor of the First Congregational Church on Central Square. The

Smiths' daughter, Dorothy June, attended the Northfield Seminary, where she began to study dramatics.

Dorothy June, or D.J., as she was known to her friends, returned to Keene for her high school years. She graduated in 1937, having been involved in the National Honor Society, student government and many other activities, especially the dramatics club.

After graduation, Dorothy June went on to study drama at Oberlin College. She continued to perform on stage and arrived in Hollywood in 1943. One month after her arrival, she was signed to a long-term contract by Universal Studios. Her first starring role was in *Honeymoon Lodge* with Ozzie and Harriet Nelson. The film opened with considerable fanfare in Keene in September 1943.

She took the stage name June Vincent and starred in nine films for Universal over the next four years. Film reviewers and historians praised her talent and lamented the fact that she was not given better roles. Her most memorable role at Universal was in the 1946 crime movie *Black Angel*, in which she tried to prove her husband innocent of murder. *Black Angel* also starred Peter Lorre and Broderick Crawford and was named as one of the top thirty film noir movies of all time.

Dorothy June was a source of great pride to Keene during the 1940s. The newspapers followed her increasing success and applauded her talent. She married a navy lieutenant in 1944 and raised a family but continued in her profession.

In the early 1950s, she also began to appear in television series and continued to do so for more than twenty-five years. She appeared in popular series such as *Rifleman*, *Perry Mason*, *Bewitched*, *The Streets of San Francisco* and *Kung Fu*. Keene's Dorothy June Smith, the June Vincent of the movies, enjoyed a long career, appearing in more than 40 movies and 150 television shows.

Chapter 6

YANKEE TALES AND
YANKEE CHARACTERS

The Legend of Granite Lake

There is a well-known legend about the history of Granite Lake, a body of water that lies in the towns of Stoddard and Nelson. This story offers us a picture of life in the region before white settlers arrived.

According to the legend, the island in the lake was at that time inhabited by an old Indian chief by the name of Pokahoket and his beautiful daughter Mamowich. One day, a handsome young Frenchman arrived at the shore of the lake while hunting and noticed the smoke from Pokahoket's campfire. He went to visit the island and was welcomed by the father and daughter.

The pair fascinated the young hunter, and he lingered by the lake, visiting the island often. Pokahoket was disabled, and the Frenchman often brought fresh game to the father and daughter. They all became close friends.

As summer gave way to autumn, Mamowich realized that she had fallen deeply in love with their handsome young friend. She waited at his campsite one evening until he returned from hunting and made her feelings known to him. The young man's surprise and embarrassment told Mamowich that her love was unrequited. The pain was too much for her to bear. She fled to her canoe, paddled quickly to the island and flung herself from its high cliffs and into the water.

The young French hunter now realized that he had stayed too long at the lake. Overcome with grief, he paddled to rescue Mamowich, but she never

The high granite ledges of the island at Granite Lake are said to be haunted by the ghost of Mamowich.

came to the surface. Pokahoket died shortly thereafter, still hoping for the return of his beautiful young daughter.

It is said that Mamowich still haunts the island and the granite ledges that rise from the cold, dark waters of Granite Lake.

GAD NEWELL OF NELSON

Gad Newell was born in Connecticut in 1763. He trained to become a saddler as a young man, but a hand injury forced him to change his career plans. He trained for the ministry at Yale, graduating in 1786. Eight years later, he was ordained to preach in Nelson, New Hampshire, at the age of thirty. He remained as the minister there for more than forty-seven years.

Newell was well known in the region for his fire-and-brimstone sermons. After he retired in the 1840s, he continued to sit in the pulpit and assist with the service each Sunday. His hearing began to deteriorate, however, and when the new pastor, the Reverend Daniel French, started his sermon, Newell would stand up beside him to be sure he could hear. Furthermore, he held an ear trumpet in front of French's face to serve as a hearing aid to

The Reverend Gad Newell preached from the pulpit in the "new" church in Nelson for the final years of his long pastorate in the town.

be sure he caught every word. The minister confided in another resident, "The hardest thing I have to do is to preach with that old ear trumpet right up in my face." The Reverend French eventually learned to accept the ear trumpet.

Gad Newell's wife, Sophia, passed away in 1840. Several years later, as he approached his ninth decade, Newell became engaged to a young woman from Keene. There was a good deal of gossip about the engagement, and many people felt that the girl was after his money. She assured everyone that she loved Gad dearly. In any case, the engagement was eventually called off, and the marriage never occurred.

In 1841, a new church was built in Nelson and the old one removed. The old church site was later used as a cemetery. Although he had officially retired from the pulpit, Newell remained active in church activities until the year he died. He passed away in 1859 at the age of ninety-five. Shortly thereafter, he and his wife were moved to the cemetery where the old church had been located. The townspeople laid Reverend Gad Newell to rest on the very spot of the old pulpit from which he had preached for almost fifty years.

Captain Kidd's Treasure

The famous pirate Captain William Kidd was executed in London in 1701 for murder and piracy. At the time of his capture, plunder amounting to less than 150 pounds of gold and silver and a few bags of jewels were seized. Most people believed that this was only a fraction of his treasure and that he had buried large amounts of booty in various locations.

Kidd had sailed into New York shortly before 1700. It was believed that he had unloaded a vast treasure and buried it in the vicinity. In the early 1820s, a rumor began in southwest New Hampshire that when Captain Kidd landed in New York, he traveled into the wilderness of southern New Hampshire. It was said that he buried some fifty pounds of gold on the shores of Rye Pond near where the towns of Antrim, Nelson and Stoddard intersect.

Many people believed this legend, and a large treasure hunt was soon underway. Hazel rods were used to try to detect the spot where the gold was buried. Local residents invested time, money and hard labor in the search. The shores of the pond were dug and dug again. No gold was found, however, and after some time passed, the excitement of buried treasure died away. The shores of the pond were quiet once again.

It seems incredible that local residents believed that Captain Kidd could have transported fifty pounds of gold through New Hampshire's uncharted wilderness to the shores of Rye Pond in 1700. But then again, most legends have some basis in fact, don't they?

SHE DIED TOO YOUNG

The widow Hannah Chapman arrived in Jaffrey with her six young children in the early 1830s. The family lived in East Jaffrey, and it was here that Hannah Jane, widow Chapman's young daughter, attended the district #2 school. By 1838, Hannah Jane was twelve years old and the prettiest girl in the school.

On June 2 of that year, the summer session was scheduled to begin. At twelve years old, Hannah could now sit with the big girls. She knew that if she got to school early on that day, she could choose her seat for the summer term. She wanted to be the first to put her books at the most popular seat under the high window where she could look down on the whole school.

She started her journey early that morning and was the first to arrive at the schoolhouse. The door was locked, however, and she was unable to claim her seat. Hannah was resourceful, however, and went to the woodshed, where she found a four-foot-long piece of wood. She propped this against the back wall of the school.

She climbed onto the wood and was able to reach the high back window. Hannah rested her books on the windowsill and raised the heavy window sash with both hands. She then held the window with one hand, took her books in the other hand, leaned way inside and dropped her books on the favorite seat.

Just at her moment of triumph, however, the piece of wood beneath Hannah's feet slipped and fell. She grasped the windowsill with both hands so that she would not fall, and the heavy window sash fell on her neck. Her lifeless body was found a short time later by two classmates who were coming to the summer term that Hannah Jane Chapman would never attend.

CAL TENNEY AND THE CATTLE DROVER

The book titled *Marlborough Recollections*, issued by the Marlborough Historical Society, contains a collection of local folktales. One of these stories concerns Calvin Tenney, a mid-nineteenth-century Marlborough tavern keeper. Calvin, born in 1792, was the twelfth child of William and Sarah Tenney, who had moved to Marlborough about twenty years earlier.

In the late 1820s, Tenney built a substantial brick house that became known as the Halfway House because it was located just halfway between

Keene and Jaffrey. This was an ideal location for a public house, and he opened a tavern there in addition to operating his farm. Tenney and his wife, Tabitha, lived in the house until the 1850s.

Much of Cal Tenney's business came from cattle drovers who stayed in the tavern at night during their cattle drives. These drovers placed their cattle in the tavern pasture in the evening, rounded them up in the morning and started on their way to the Boston market. Cal charged a nominal amount per head for the pasturing and safekeeping.

One day, a drover stopped off at the tavern to spend the night. He knew of the fee for pasturing cattle but was not anxious to part with his money. The man put his herd into the pasture, went up to the tavern and told Cal that he had already pastured his 125 cattle. Cal, who had been watching from the window, said that was fine.

The next morning after breakfast, the drover paid his bill, including the charge for 125 cattle. "I'll go down with you while you get your herd," Cal said. He opened the pasture gate and watched the cattle come through. When 125 head of cattle had passed, Cal closed the gate. The drover pointed out that a good number of the cattle still in the pasture were his. Cal replied, "I counted out 125 cattle. That's the number you [told] me and paid me for. The rest of them critters must be mine."

The drover knew he had been caught and he had to pay the fee for the rest of his cattle, including a fine—a round of drinks for everyone in the tavern.

Thunder over Stoddard

Thoughts of the summer thunderstorm season recall the story of Nancy Messenger. Nancy was born in Stoddard, New Hampshire, in 1806. Twenty-three years later, she married Marshall Messenger in December 1829.

During the next five years, the couple built a farm and began a family in the wild northeast corner of Stoddard. Marshall cleared the fields, and the family could look down toward the series of ponds that later became Highland Lake.

On the morning of a beautiful July day in 1835, Marshall and a hired hand left the house early and went out to cut hay in a field near the house. Nancy and the couple's two children—Anna, age four, and Hattie, age two—stayed at the house. Toward the middle of the day, several clouds overhead thickened into one. Marshall soon saw a flash of lightning that streaked toward the house.

The two men ran from the field to the farmhouse. The neighbors also came running. When they arrived, they found Marshall sitting in the doorway with Nancy lying dead in his arms and their two sobbing daughters clinging to either side.

Marshall remarried one year later, and Anna and Hattie grew up and had families of their own. Today, the Messenger house and barns have been gone for more than a century. The fields have grown back to forest. Only the cellar hole and stone walls offer proof that Marshall and Nancy lived there.

The story of Nancy's sad end has not been forgotten, however. The names given to two hills not far from the site of the family farmhouse remind today's residents of this tragedy; one is named Nancy Mountain, and the other is Lightning Hill.

Guarding the Grave

David Smith and his wife, Lucy, came to Gilsum from Gardner, Massachusetts, in about 1815. The Smiths purchased a tavern and blacksmith shop and began a family. David became active in church and town affairs, serving as tithingman and sexton.

One day in March 1825, David went up to the Vessel Rock neighborhood to help a neighbor with a house-raising. During the raising of the house frame, a beam fell, killing him instantly. Because he died in sound health, it was feared that grave robbers would attempt to snatch his body for use at a medical college.

This was a time when grave robbing was not uncommon; the bodies were used for dissection and medical education. A highly publicized case of body snatching had occurred in nearby Acworth just four months earlier, undoubtedly adding to the Smith family's fears.

Consequently, the family decided to place guards at David's grave. The guards reported that several people approached the cemetery from different directions but quickly drove away when they found someone there.

Watching the grave became so time consuming that the body was disinterred and buried under the wood pile in the Smith family's yard. The fears of grave robbing were apparently well founded. When David's body was eventually returned to the grave in the cemetery, it was found that a log that had been placed in the grave in his place had been moved.

Despite all these difficulties, David Smith of Gilsum was returned to, and remained in, his final resting place.

Bedbug Point

Being a schoolteacher was not an easy job in the mid-1800s. In addition to preparing lessons and teaching classes, teachers usually had to shovel the snow, chop the wood and stoke the fire. They often had to clean the classroom as well.

Teachers were not paid very well either, especially women, who received about half the pay of male teachers. Finally, if schoolteachers did not live in the town where they were teaching, they had to board with a family of strangers.

On top of these responsibilities, one Westmoreland teacher found yet another difficulty to contend with, for which she is remembered to the present day. Local legend says that the schoolmarm at the District Nine School in Westmoreland was boarding at a nearby farmhouse. Soon after arriving at the house, the teacher found that her room was infested with bedbugs. She mentioned this to the farmer's wife, who assured the young schoolmarm that she certainly must be mistaken. One morning, after another night with the bedbugs, the teacher impaled several of the creatures on pins and laid them on the bureau as proof of her claim.

The District Nine School remains today as a museum and home of the Westmoreland Historical Society. The bedbugs are surely long gone, but their story is well known in Westmoreland; some residents still refer to that neighborhood as Bedbug Point.

The Battle of the Banners

More than 170 years ago, southwest New Hampshire experienced a season of very competitive and spirited political electioneering. The presidential campaign of 1852 generated a great deal of interest and excitement locally because of the nomination of New Hampshire's own Franklin Pierce by the Democratic Party.

The presidential contest aroused the spirit of competition between Keene's Democrats and the town's Whigs, whose party had nominated Winfield Scott for the presidency. It was during this campaign that the practice of displaying flags with the candidates' names came into common use. The Whigs erected a flagpole over the *New Hampshire Sentinel* newspaper building on Central Square on which they flew a flag with the names of Scott and his running mate William A. Graham. This aroused the Democrats, who erected a larger staff over the *Cheshire Republican* news office on the opposite side of Central Square. From this pole they displayed a larger flag with the names of candidate and New Hampshire native Franklin Pierce and his running mate, William King.

The Whigs then spliced their pole, making it several feet taller than the one erected by the Democrats, and flew a new and larger flag. This move prompted their opponents to cut a spruce tree almost eighty feet tall. They raised this as a flagpole and ran up the largest flag ever flown in Keene to that time.

The Whigs were not to be outdone, however. They took to the woods in search of a taller tree. They found one in Sullivan that was over one hundred feet tall. It was cut down, hewn and decorated there in the woods. A gilded eagle was fastened to its top, and a hole was cut through the roof of the *Sentinel* building so that the new flagstaff could be erected. The tree was raised and the big end fastened to the attic floor. The pole rose more than ninety feet above the top of the roof. A flag fifty by thirty feet in size emblazoned with the names Scott and Graham, and topped by a streamer one hundred feet long, flew from the top.

The battle of the banners held the attention of the townspeople for several weeks. The Whigs won the battle with their fifty-by-thirty-foot flag. They lost the war, however, as the Democratic candidate, Franklin Pierce, won the presidency.

THE PONY EXPRESS CONNECTION

George Henry Scovell was born in Walpole, New Hampshire, three days after Christmas in the year 1838. He grew up in the town, probably spending many hours at his grandfather's prosperous farm.

Scovell ran away from home at age eighteen. He first went to Nebraska, where he took up a tract of government land. He was underage, however, and could not gain proper title to the land. Claim jumpers appropriated the property. Scovell then went on to Salt Lake City, where he took a job with the Pony Express. Being underage and hoping to hide his identity, he went only by the name of "Boston."

Scovell rode the 525-mile Pony Express route from Salt Lake City to Virginia City. He had several encounters with Indians during his time in the West. On one trip, he was ambushed and one of his attackers tried to disable Scovell's horse with his tomahawk. The blow hit the stirrup, however, and inflicted a serious wound to Scovell's foot. The chase continued for several miles, during which time he was further weakened by two arrows in his hand. He finally reached safety at the next mail station, where his horse died because of its many arrow wounds. Scovell soon moved on to Sacramento, California, where he drove a 50-mile stage route on the Overland Stage Line.

He returned in 1872 to New England, where he married Carrie Mason, his childhood neighbor from Walpole. The couple moved to Wakefield, Massachusetts, and he eventually sold butter from a cart at Faneuil Hall in Boston.

He never forgot his time with the Pony Express, however. Scovell kept a diary during those years and gave lectures on his experiences. George Henry Scovell, Walpole's Pony Express rider, passed away in Wakefield in 1916.

THE BARKER BLOCK LOTTERY

The attractive French Second Empire–style Barker Block at the corner of Court and Center Streets in Keene was constructed for Fred A. Barker in 1870. The new block, constructed at a cost of about $15,000, contained seven separate residential units. These were to be sold separately in what was probably Keene's first true condominium.

The Barker Block, Keene's first condominium, soon after it was built in 1870.

Barker devised a clever plan to conduct a lottery as a means of disposing of the property. Tickets cost one dollar each. The winners of the units were to be drawn at a grand musical jubilee at the town hall on March 23, 1871. Posters prominently displayed throughout the town described the ten-room units as having "all the modern improvements" and being in the "most desirable location in Keene." There was also a common courtyard at the rear of the building.

The musical jubilee took place as planned, but only one-fourth of the tickets were sold. Consequently, only one and a half units were to be given away as prizes. The *New Hampshire Sentinel* reported that the whole unit was drawn by a man from Laconia and the half tenement by a resident of Milford.

Unfortunately, the lottery was declared illegal by the police department. The money was returned, and Barker was fined thirty dollars on two separate counts of selling an illegal lottery ticket. Barker then proceeded to sell the units individually. The Barker Block still stands today, housing offices and apartments, more than 150 years after it was raffled off by Fred Barker.

93RD STREET

Many residents know that Keene has a street named 93rd Street. However, many residents do not know that this is Keene's only street with a number for a name, nor do they know how the name came about.

In the mid-1870s, William Brooks's blacksmith shop stood behind his Church Street home in a location between Railroad and Church Streets. Brooks advertised that he did horse and ox shoeing and general blacksmithing and that he made tools for stone working.

The entrance to the shop was a lane through the yard of a neighboring machine shop. Brooks felt that his business would increase if a street went directly past his shop. To help his idea along, he obtained the signatures of fifty-nine people on a petition to the city asking that a street be built there.

There was a good deal of opposition to the street, however. An opposing petition, with the names of ninety-three dissenters, was brought before the city council, and the new street was refused. Brooks would not give up the fight, however. He presented such favorable arguments to the city that the street was finally approved.

The following day, Brooks placed a hand-painted sign bearing the name "93rd Street" on the site where the street would be located. To show his pleasure with the council's decision, he had personally named the future street for the number of people who had opposed its construction. When the street was officially laid out in December 1875, the name stuck, and 93rd Street became Keene's newest street. William Brooks had discontinued his blacksmith shop by 1900, but the street remains more than 140 years later as Keene's only numbered street.

Arsenic and Old Flannel

In March 1889, a local newspaper reported on an unusual case of arsenic poisoning. Miss Bessie Blake, daughter of Keene farmer Milton Blake, had been very ill for two weeks. Dr. George Twitchell of Keene felt that the seventeen-year-old Bessie had unmistakable symptoms of arsenic poisoning. No one could determine the origin of the illness, however.

At first, Dr. Twitchell suspected the wallpaper in Bessie's room. Keene High School principal Charles Douglas inspected a piece of the paper but found no trace of arsenic. Finally, Bessie's grandmother suggested that a new dress that Bessie had recently made and worn might be the cause of the trouble. The dress was made of green flannel. School principal Douglas was called in once again to do a test. Upon examination, he found that the flannel contained arsenic.

There was no explanation in the newspaper as to how the arsenic got into the flannel. A few decades earlier, however, dress makers had determined that arsenic could be used to dye cloth green. They did not know, or did not care, that the arsenic in the cloth could be very poisonous to those who bought and wore the dresses made from the cloth.

The government was not monitoring the use of chemicals closely in 1889 if a flannel dress could contain enough arsenic to make the person wearing it seriously ill. Thanks to the investigations carried out by Dr. Twitchell and school principal Douglas in Keene, young Bessie Blake's dress was discarded, and she recovered from her bout of arsenic poisoning.

The Frugal Yankee

Ed Shedd was well known as the most frugal Yankee farmer in his hometown of Stoddard, New Hampshire. Born in Stoddard in 1849, he lived on the family farm the rest of his life.

Frugal Yankee Ed Shedd posed outside his Stoddard farmhouse.

Ed owned a good deal of property and was quite well off, but you would not have known it by looking at him. He did not spend money unless he had to, including money for new clothes. Whenever he had business to transact, he would walk many miles to Keene, Milford or wherever he had to go. He saw no reason to spend a dollar on a train or stagecoach ride when he could walk.

One time, Ed walked into Keene to deposit $3,000 in the bank, but by the time he got there, the bank was closed. Rather than renting a room, he sat on a park bench in Keene's Central Square with his hand in his pocket wrapped around his roll of money until the bank opened the next morning.

On another occasion, he hiked into Keene to deposit another $1,500 in the bank. The story is that two highwaymen heard of this and lay in wait for him just outside the city. When Ed trudged into sight, they thought he was a tramp and let him pass unmolested. The two robbers soon stopped a well-dressed fellow who came along and got the fifteen cents he was carrying.

Ed once walked to California to see more of the world. He put $100 in each sock to cover expenses. When he got home the next spring, he had $200 in each sock! He was in a public place after his return home when he overheard a woman saying she wanted to go to California but could not afford to. He turned to her and suggested that she could walk because, after all, he had made the trip successfully on foot.

Ed suffered a broken leg in his later years and spent some time in the Keene hospital. He returned home after recovering, but soon missed the care and attention of the nurses so much that he returned to the hospital and spent the final four years of his life there. He insisted on paying his hospital bill every day. When he passed away at age eighty-five in 1934, Ed Shedd of Stoddard left his entire estate, nearly $55,000, to the Elliot Community Hospital of Keene.

Wilder's Warning

Eugene Wilder was born in Alstead in 1860. His father, Henry, died of disease five years later while serving in the Civil War. Gene and his mother, Ann, remained in Alstead, where he worked to support the family and eventually operated a farm on Forest Road.

In addition to farming, Gene also became sexton of the town cemeteries in Alstead. Huge pine trees in the West Yard shaded many of the lots in that cemetery. By 1908, the town was debating whether some of the trees should be cut. Sexton Wilder particularly disliked the trees. "Right kind of weather come along, these trees will flat every headstone here," he said. "Me, when I'm underground, I'll go out in the new part where the sun'll keep me warm." The trees remained despite his warning.

Gene Wilder died in January 1938 at the age of seventy-seven. Despite his desire to be buried out in the sun, he was buried under the great pines beside his wife. Seven months later, the hurricane of 1938 struck the area. Although a dozen of the large pine trees were blown down by the wind, only one headstone was broken. It was Gene Wilder's.

Amos Potter, Adventurer

Amos Potter was born in Jaffrey, New Hampshire, in October 1874. Young Amos had an eye for adventure, perhaps inspired by tales of his father serving and being wounded in the Civil War. When he was still in his late teens, Amos left home and traveled across the country to Seattle. He then went in search of gold at Butte, Montana, when that community was a wild, rowdy mining town.

Amos followed the gold camps through Colorado and Nevada and eventually crossed the border into Mexico. After working there for two years, his mining camp was raided by Pancho Villa and his Mexican bandits. Of the eighteen Americans in the camp, only Amos and one other were left alive after the raid.

The two agreed to join the bandits to save their lives. The two men escaped one night while on picket duty after four years with the rebels. They managed to cross the border into the United States just before General Pershing's expedition went into Mexico to punish the bandits. Amos tried to join the American forces but could not pass the physical exam.

At the beginning of World War I, he went to Los Angeles and tried to join the army but was rejected once again. Consequently, Amos worked at a TNT munitions plant in that city throughout the war.

Amos wrote to his family in Jaffrey after the war ended. He told them he was about to begin a gold prospecting expedition to Alaska. That was the last that anyone in the Potter family ever heard from Jaffrey's adventurous Amos Potter.

Chapter 7

EMPOWERED WOMEN

MARTHA ALDRICH AND THE WOLF

Martha and Nathan Aldrich were early settlers of Richmond, New Hampshire, arriving there around 1770. They lived in the northeast part of town on the road to Swanzey. Wolves were still common in the region at that time, and one of them began visiting the Aldrich farm and upsetting the livestock.

In the spring of 1771, Nathan had to make an extended trip to his native town of Mendon, Massachusetts. He was concerned that the wolf might make another visit during his absence. A young man named Daniel Peters was living with the Aldrich family at that time, and Nathan gave him very specific instructions about what to do if the wolf returned. Nathan gave detailed instructions on how to load the gun, where to keep it and how to use it. Nathan's small but spunky dog was left at the house in case he might be of some assistance.

Soon after Nathan left the farm, Martha and young Daniel were aroused by frantic barking by the small dog. They looked out to find the dog being chased into the yard by the wolf. The wolf caught the dog, and the two began to fight. The small dog was clearly overmatched, and Martha instructed the youngster to shoot the wolf. Daniel was either too scared or too nervous, however, and Martha could not convince him to make the shot.

Martha took control of the situation to try to save the small dog. She picked up her heavy birch-handled broom and ran across the yard, swinging the broom over her head while screaming at the wolf. The animal was so startled that it abandoned the fight and ran into the woods. The dog was badly wounded but eventually recovered. The small canine was cherished by the family thereafter for the strength that he displayed during the fight with the wolf.

Poor Daniel Peters did not fare so well, however. His reputation was tarnished by his inaction during the confrontation. Not only did he move to another part of town, but he was entirely dismissed by the young woman who had favorably been receiving his attentions before the wolf interfered.

ADVERTISING WIVES

It was a common practice among our ancestors to advertise a runaway spouse in the newspaper. A husband would buy an advertisement stating that his wife had run away so that no one would allow her credit in his name. This practice was most common in Cheshire County newspapers in the late 1700s. In the early 1800s, John Prentiss published a notice that he would no longer allow these advertisements in his *New Hampshire Sentinel*, but they continued to appear in the paper as late as 1819.

These ads often offered amusing accounts of domestic problems for the whole world to see. Joseph Davis of Chesterfield placed the following ad in the *New Hampshire Recorder* in November 1787: "Where as my wife Margaret has eloped from my bed and board and refuses living with me. This is to forbid all persons trusting her on my account."

This upset Margaret, who responded with an ad of her own. It was published two weeks later and read as follows:

> *Where as my husband, Joseph Davis, has informed the public that I have eloped from HIS bed and board, I beg leave to inform the public that he has not been the possessor of either since I was married to him, the 1st of August, 1786. That I have supported him and his daughter since that time....That he took 14 pounds of my money to purchase clothing for himself without leaving me one farthing. And that there was no danger of my running him into debt as his credit was insufficient for that purpose.*

We often know very little about local female residents of the eighteenth century. We know about Margaret Davis, however, a strong woman who was going to be heard and who got her point across more effectively than her husband.

Cherokee Sisters

During the 1830s, the United States government was in the process of forcing the Cherokee Indians to leave their homes east of the Mississippi River and move westward to a new wild and unimproved reservation. The Cherokees sent some prominent men of their tribe to Washington to plead for their homes, without success.

One of these men, a Mr. Field, also asked for help with the education of the young people in the tribe who were eager to learn. Mary Parker, a teacher at the new Keene Academy, read about this plea. She sent word that if one of these Indian girls would come to Keene, she would provide them with a home and an education at the academy.

Elizabeth Field, one of the daughters of the Mr. Field who had been in Washington, came to Keene. She moved into the Court Street home of Elijah Parker, Mary's father. Elizabeth entered the academy immediately.

After a year in Keene, she begged that her sister Amanda might join her. Amanda soon arrived in the town also, moved in with the Parkers and entered the academy. Amanda was much more lighthearted and cheerful than her proper and elegant sister Elizabeth.

The Cherokee sisters made a fine impression in the town and spent at least two more years here together completing their studies at the academy. They then returned home to the Cherokee nation.

The girls corresponded with the Parker family for many years. Both married U.S. Army officers. Amanda died quite young, in the late 1840s. Elizabeth died some twenty years later. Both girls left families, and both left friends in Keene, where they had received their formal education far from the Cherokee Reservation.

Hannah's Bandboxes

Hannah Davis, born in 1784, was the daughter of Peter Davis, a skilled maker of wooden clocks. The Davises lived in Jaffrey, New Hampshire.

Hannah's father died when she was quite young, and Hannah stayed with her mother until her mother died in 1818. Hannah never married, and she now needed a means of support.

Having grown up in a family of woodworkers, Hannah turned to wood for her livelihood. She began to make and sell bandboxes. Her bandboxes were round or oval wooden boxes made of spruce and pine and covered with colorful wallpaper. The boxes were large enough for hats, shoes and other clothing and household items. They were used for storage in the home or during travel.

Hannah picked out the spruce trees and made the boxes herself. She would then trade them with local merchants for tea, sugar and whatever she needed from the store. Her boxes became popular, and the business grew.

Hannah would load a canvas-covered wagon with bandboxes and drive to the mills at Manchester and Lowell. During the lunch break, the mill girls would eagerly buy the bandboxes at prices ranging from twelve to fifty cents each. She made her boxes for many years before she retired. "Aunt Hannah," as the town residents called her, passed away in 1863.

Hannah Davis bandboxes are eagerly sought by antique collectors, who now pay a good deal more than the original fifty cents. These boxes are collectible not only because they are rare antiques but also because Hannah Davis was one of the first successful businesswomen who offered a product for women, made by a woman.

THANKS TO SARAH

Although we often associate Thanksgiving Day with the Pilgrim settlers of Massachusetts, it has been an official holiday only since the 1860s. Sarah Josepha Hale of Newport, New Hampshire, played a major role in making this day one of our most important national holidays.

Sarah was born in Newport, then part of Cheshire County, in 1788. She grew up there, attended local schools and studied her brother's college textbooks to learn Latin, philosophy and advanced mathematics. In 1813, she married David Hale, brother of Keene's well-known historian Salma Hale. Nine years later, David died, leaving Sarah to support a family of five children. She taught school and began to write. Realizing the importance of education, she sent her daughters to study at Catherine Fiske's Young Ladies Seminary in Keene.

After publishing a successful novel in 1827, Sarah was invited to become editor of a ladies' magazine that later became *Godey's Lady's Book*. As the first woman editor of a national magazine, Sarah used her influence to aid various charities and improve the status of women in this country.

She wrote about fifty books during her lifetime. She also worked to preserve Washington's Mount Vernon home and raised funds for the construction of the Bunker Hill Monument. One of her most famous causes, however, was the Thanksgiving holiday.

In the mid-1840s, Sarah suggested that there should be a national holiday of Thanksgiving to honor our forefathers and recognize the bounty of our nation. No one was against Thanksgiving, but the states wanted to name their own day. As a result, the date of the holiday differed from year to year and state to state. Furthermore, Thanksgiving was chiefly a New England holiday, with few southern states celebrating the day.

For nearly twenty years, Sarah wrote editorials and letters to governors and presidents calling for an official holiday. After writing to Presidents Taylor, Fillmore, Pierce and Buchanan, Sarah wrote to President Lincoln. Finally, in 1863, President Abraham Lincoln declared the last Thursday in November a national Thanksgiving Day holiday. At seventy-five years old, Sarah Josepha Hale of Newport had won her long battle and is remembered today as the "Mother of Thanksgiving."

Carrie Cutter's War

Carrie E. Cutter has been described as the "beautiful and accomplished daughter" of Dr. Calvin Cutter of Jaffrey, New Hampshire. Calvin, born in Jaffrey in 1807, was an accomplished surgeon, lecturer and author. Daughter Carrie attended private schools and displayed a special aptitude for languages, including German. She also accompanied and assisted her father when he visited patients. The Cutter family lived in Warren, Massachusetts, by the time the Civil War began in 1861.

Dr. Cutter was appointed surgeon of the Twenty-First Massachusetts Infantry during the war. When nineteen-year-old Carrie asked what she could do to help the cause, she was told to stay home and keep house because the war was no place for women. As her father prepared for service, Carrie organized soldiers' aid societies throughout Massachusetts and furnished complete hospital supplies to her father's regiment and the entire second brigade of Sherman's expedition to Port Royal.

In October 1861, Dr. Cutter was ordered to sail with Burnside's expedition to Roanoke, Virginia. Carrie refused to remain behind at home and petitioned the government to allow her to accompany her father. Her petition was eventually approved, and she was allowed to sail on Dr. Cutter's troop ship as his nurse.

A battle was fought when the ship arrived at Roanoke, and Carrie worked alongside her father providing care for the wounded. When the battle ended, the pair went ashore to offer further assistance. Carrie was soon exhausted but came across three German soldiers who could not speak English. Despite her weakened condition, she was allowed to care for the three because of her proficiency in German. She worked day and night until the trio began to recover. She was entirely exhausted by this time, however, and, in her weakened state, was stricken with typhoid fever. Young Carrie had little strength to fight the fever and died in the cabin of her father's ship soon after contracting the disease.

General Burnside ordered that she be buried with military honors. When the National Cemetery was established at New Bern, North Carolina, the secretary of war directed that Carrie be moved to that cemetery and buried with the soldiers for whom she had sacrificed her life. New Hampshire's Carrie Cutter was one of the first women to give her life in the Civil War and one of the first to be buried in a national cemetery. Her name is included on the Roll of Honor in the Library of Congress in Washington, D.C.

CHAPLAIN ELLA GIBSON

Ella Elvira Gibson was born in Winchendon, Massachusetts, in May 1821. The Gibson family moved to Rindge when Ella was five years old. She spent the remainder of her childhood there on the family farm, attended local schools and began to teach in the schools herself at age fifteen.

Ella was forced to give up teaching at age twenty-seven due to illness, and she began to lecture and write. She wrote articles for the *Boston Cultivator*, and by the early 1860s, she was delivering hundreds of lectures annually across the country. She would speak without preparation on topics chosen by the audience or on subjects dealing with reform. Ella was lecturing in the West when the Civil War began. She offered her services to start soldiers' aid societies and raise money for the Sanitary Commission.

Ella married the Reverend John Hobart in Geneva, Wisconsin, in 1861. Later that year, Hobart was elected chaplain of the Eighth Wisconsin

Regiment. Ella accompanied her husband to the front, where she assisted him with his duties and nursed sick and wounded soldiers. The couple separated in 1864, and Ella went to Wisconsin's secretary of state to seek a chaplain's job for herself. She was advised to apply for the chaplaincy of the First Wisconsin Heavy Artillery. She was elected to that post by the men of the regiment and began her service with the military.

The colonel of the regiment asked the governor of Wisconsin to commission Ella. The governor felt that he could not do this because, as a female, Ella was not officially eligible for the post. The request was sent on to Secretary of War Edwin Stanton. Stanton conferred with President Lincoln, who wrote that he had no legal standing in the matter but had no objection to the appointment. Stanton did not wish to set a precedent, however, by commissioning a female chaplain in the army and simply did not reply to the request. In the end, Ella simply served as chaplain without being mustered into the military.

For years after the war, she fought to receive her chaplain's pay and a pension for her service. She finally received $1,200 in pay but was never awarded a pension. She became embittered by her lack of recognition and returned to Massachusetts to live with her widowed sister. Although she did not receive recognition in her lifetime, Rindge's Ella Gibson is generally recognized today as the first female chaplain in the U.S. Army.

Mary's Hospital

Mary Maynard was born in the Walpole, New Hampshire village of Drewsville in 1834. She was the daughter of John Maynard, who operated a tannery there. When Mary was eight years old, Jesse Hitchcock moved his family from Claremont to the village of Drewsville. Jesse's youngest son was named Hiram. Mary and Hiram met as youngsters and grew up together in Drewsville. The two were married in 1858.

Prior to their marriage, Hiram had worked for several years in the hotel business in New Orleans and Massachusetts. Following the marriage, the two moved to New York, where Hiram established the Fifth Avenue Hotel with two partners. Income from the hotel soon made Hiram and Mary very wealthy. Hiram retired from active management of the hotel in 1866.

The couple traveled for several years and moved to Hanover, New Hampshire, in 1870. They spent seventeen years there at their home beside the Connecticut River before Mary passed away in 1887.

Hiram immediately decided to build a hospital in Hanover in her memory. He personally oversaw the construction, and the state-of-the-art hospital was completed in 1893. A bronze plaque was placed in the administration building and inscribed in memory of Mary and "her tender and unfailing sympathy for the afflicted and poor." The "tender sympathies" of Drewsville's Mary Hitchcock have been memorialized for more than one hundred years at Hanover's Mary Hitchcock Memorial Hospital, more recently known as the DartmouthHitchcock Medical Center.

Lone Star May

Mary Mackey was born in Keene on October 21, 1873. Her parents, Michael and Amelia, both natives of Nova Scotia, had purchased a lot of land on Chapman Road at a land auction on August 1 of that year. They immediately began to build a house there and moved in before snow fell, so Mary's birth may have been one of the first family events in the new house.

The Mackey home was a small but busy one. The family eventually had fifteen children, several of whom did not survive to adulthood. The upstairs of the home was divided into two large sleeping rooms—one for the girls and one for the boys. This caring but crowded setting was where Mary grew up.

She was described as tempestuous and rather wild by a contemporary. Her strong personality and the cramped setting at home may have played a role in her leaving at an early age. Mary traveled west, and by the 1890s, she had secured a part in one of the popular Wild West shows of the day. She was a crack shot and an excellent trick rider.

Mary took the professional name Lone Star May. She won shooting competitions, including the California Fruit Growers Association Rifle Match in 1893. Her family claimed that she never missed when shooting at clay pigeons. Showgirl Lone Star May claimed she was from Texas for the purposes of the show. Several pictures of Mary in show costume with rifle in hand and on horseback have survived. One photo of twenty-year-old Mary shows a slim young woman in an old West–style dress wearing a cowboy hat and holding the Krag-Jorgensen rifle that she had just won as first prize in the California Fruit Growers competition.

Lone Star May traveled the country with the Wild West shows, exhibiting her skills and living on her own terms. She returned to Keene to visit only a few times after she left. Perhaps she was with Buffalo Bill's Wild West

Show when it appeared in Keene in 1908. She was a contemporary, and may have been a friend, of Phoebe Ann Mosey, better known as famed sharpshooter Annie Oakley. It may have been Mary whom Annie Oakley came to call on when the *Keene Sentinel* reported she was in Keene to visit friends in June 1916.

Mary Mackey, Lone Star May, was certainly one of Keene's early empowered women, striking out on her own at a young age and making a career in a field usually reserved for men. Mary did not return to Keene to live after her career ended. She passed away in San Antonio, Texas, in the state that she had always claimed was her home.

Ladies Wildwood Park

Caroline Haskell Ingersoll was born in 1827 to a member of a prominent Keene family. Her grandfather was a veteran of the Revolutionary War and served as commandant at West Point. Her father, George, was minister for many years before retiring to the family's large home in Keene in 1849.

Caroline never married and remained in Keene the rest of her life, where she became involved in local causes. In 1886, she learned that a pine grove

The entrance to Ladies Wild Wood Park. The land for the park was saved through donations made by the ladies of Keene.

near her family home in West Keene was about to be cut down for timber. She immediately went to work to preserve the grove for use as a public park.

The price for the parcel was $1,300. She decided to ask the ladies of Keene to support the effort to preserve the land for public use. By December 1886, Caroline had raised $550 from twenty-five women toward the effort. The list of donors included the names of many of the city's well-known families, including Ball, Colony, Dort, Elliot, Faulkner, Griffin, Joslin and Thayer.

Local newspapers began to publicize the fundraising effort; by January 1887, Caroline was within $200 of her goal. She announced that the park would receive the name Ladies Park because most of the funds to purchase the land had come from the ladies of the community. By March, the fundraising was complete. More than one hundred donors had contributed the money for the purchase. One additional donor gave $100 for the care and upkeep of the park.

In May 1887, the seventeen-acre parcel was donated to the city on behalf of the donors. The city was charged with holding the land forever for use as a "public pleasure ground or Wild Wood park." Furthermore, no trees were to be removed unless necessary for trails or to maintain the health of the forest. The donors prepared walking trails, placed inscribed boulders at the entrances to the park and installed a drinking fountain and several benches.

Caroline asked that the park be overseen by several of the female donors for a period of twenty-five years, after which it would become the responsibility of the city. She also made an annual gift for the maintenance of the park.

Upon the conveyance of the land to the city, the new park was given the name Ladies Wildwood Park. The park was later enlarged by the gift of two additional parcels. The city park remains today at the intersection of Arch Street and Park Avenue. Thanks to Caroline Ingersoll, Ladies Wildwood Park is still available today for walking, relaxation and, as she expressed, "public pleasure" for the residents of Keene.

JENNIE POWERS, THE WOMAN WHO DARED

Jennie B. Carter was born in Brattleboro, Vermont, in 1864. She graduated from Brattleboro High School and went on to study taxidermy and bird life. She married Frank Powers in the 1880s, and by the 1890s, Jennie was working as a humane society agent for Windham County, Vermont. In

Humane society agent and Cheshire County deputy sheriff Jennie B. Powers feeding calves in Keene.

1903, she became the agent for the Keene Humane Society with jurisdiction throughout Cheshire County.

The mission of the Keene Humane Society was to protect animals, children and women from abuse and neglect. Humane societies at the time were charged with helping people as well as animals. Jennie was deputized by the county sheriff in 1910. As an empowered deputy, she investigated thousands of cases of abuse, arresting offenders, prosecuting court cases and upholding early cruelty laws. Jennie Powers was a heroic agent of change during a time when women were just beginning to push for rights to vote, to control property and to have a legal say over the welfare of their own children. Her tenacity and compassion were well known nationally.

Newspapers of the time included numerous stories of Powers confronting farmers, loggers and livestock shippers, demanding that they cease mistreatment of cattle and horses. It is said that she once jumped from a window of her home to stop a man from beating his horses. A major focus of Powers's activism was the inspection of cattle being shipped through Keene by train. At the freight yards, she inspected cattle for illness, intervening when needed and even feeding them herself.

In an age when animal cruelty laws were more defined than laws against family violence, much of Powers's work led her to protect the rights of children and wives who were abused and neglected. Her work could be dangerous; she often received threats from those who had been prosecuted for cruelty. She carried a .44-caliber revolver on her hip and slept with it under her pillow.

On January 4, 1918, the *Vermont Phoenix* newspaper reported, "Mrs. Powers' work on behalf of suffering children has given her a front place in the ranks of humanitarians. She has gone into rough logging camps miles away from any village, into the homes of outlaws, where male officers feared to go, making her own arrests, sometimes at the point of a revolver, and then prosecuting the cases in court." Jennie Powers was a Progressive Era leader who bravely stood up against social vices in New Hampshire and Vermont in the early twentieth century. She remained active in her work until her death in Keene in 1936.

Her work has not gone unrecognized. In 1967, the Monadnock Humane Society named its present site the Jennie B. Powers Memorial Shelter in her honor, and in 2019, the Jennie Powers story was chosen as one of sixteen Keene Walldogs mural topics selected to illustrate the history of the city of Keene.

AMELIA EARHART IN KEENE

Amelia Earhart was a heroine to American women of the 1930s. She was attractive, intelligent and, most importantly, a huge success in the male-dominated field of aviation. During 1928, Earhart was the first female passenger on a transatlantic flight. Four years later, in 1932, she became the first woman to fly across the Atlantic Ocean alone and immediately became a national celebrity.

In November 1932, shortly after she completed her historic flight, she came to Keene to tell the story of her adventure. On the evening of November 15, Earhart spoke to a large audience at the Colonial Theatre on Main Street. She was described by a *Keene Sentinel* reporter as "tall and slender, perfectly at ease, and better looking than many of her pictures."

Earhart spoke for an hour and a half, describing in detail her flight across the Atlantic. She told the crowd that her flight began at Teterboro, New Jersey. She flew through storms and had instrument problems but finally landed in a farmer's field near Londonderry, Ireland. From Ireland, she made a victory tour of Europe, stopping at London, Paris, Brussels and Rome.

Earhart predicted that anyone in her audience in Keene who had not flown in an airplane would do so within two years. Her speech here was a great success and did much to help convince the local citizens of the growing importance of aviation. Less than five years after her visit to Keene, she attempted to fly around the world. During that flight, on July 3, 1937, her plane vanished over the ocean, and Amelia Earhart was never seen again.

Chapter 8

CRIME AND PUNISHMENT

THE EVIL DOCTOR

In June 1815, a pompous-looking fellow calling himself the famous Dr. Dexter arrived at Sumner's Tavern in downtown Keene. On the day that he arrived, he advertised in the *New Hampshire Sentinel* inviting local citizens to visit him at the tavern to receive treatment for their illnesses.

Among the twenty-two specialties that he listed in the advertisement were cancer, jaundice, tapeworms, whooping cough, dysentery, deafness and female diseases of all descriptions. He claimed he had studied with Indian, German and French botanists for more than five years and had been in practice for thirteen years. Dr. Dexter soon had a waiting list of patients and decided to stay in the region. He soon moved his practice to his home near the meetinghouse in Roxbury.

In October 1816, Dexter was brought to trial in Keene on a charge of malpractice. In the fall of 1815, he had examined a sore on the ankle of one Pedda Day. Dexter diagnosed the sore as cancer and said that he could cure it. He applied a caustic that destroyed the flesh and muscles to the bone. When cutting out the sore, he also cut tendons and destroyed the use of Pedda's foot. Dr. Amos Twitchell testified at the trial that a true doctor would have realized that the sore was not cancer and that the treatment was very improper.

Pedda Day was awarded $400 by the jury. This must have damaged Dexter's practice, but it was surely ruined two months later when the *Sentinel* reported that three years earlier, he had lived in Buffalo, New York, where he was known as Luther Gothro, a shoemaker. Furthermore, he left Buffalo just before he was to stand trial for criminal misconduct.

Pedda Day died in Chesterfield six months later, but history has not recorded what became of John Dexter. It was cases like this one, however, that resulted in laws governing the training and qualifications of those practicing medicine and surgery.

HORSE THIEF–DETECTING SOCIETIES

Our ancestors set up their own system of discouraging crime long before the neighborhood watch system was organized in the twentieth century. As early as 1816, Cheshire County residents were forming local horse thief–detecting societies. Both the Keene and Marlborough societies were formed in the 1830s. The Walpole society may have had the longest name; it was known as the Walpole Society for Detecting and Punishing Horse Thieves and Pilferers and Plunderers of Gardens and Fruit Orchards.

The purpose of these organizations was to bring to justice horse thieves and recover stolen horses. Some of the organizations later extended their

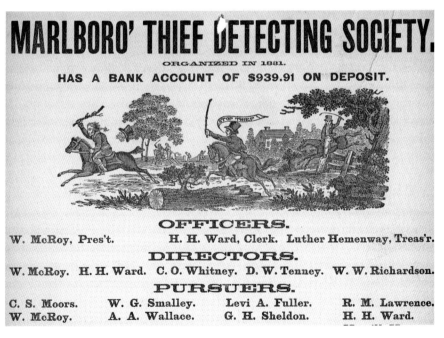

The Marlborough Horse Thief–Detecting Society was one of several such crime prevention and detection societies in the region.

watchful coverage to protecting gardens, orchards and other commonly plundered or stolen items.

Any resident of the town where the organization was located could become a member by paying annual dues. Should any member have a horse or other property stolen, he could apply to the society to send out riders to pursue the horse and the thief, to advertise the theft and to offer a reward for the return of the property.

The records of local horse thief–detecting societies show that riders, or pursuers, as they were sometimes called, were indeed paid for expenses incurred in apprehending thieves and recovering property. Rewards were also paid; Milton Carter of Peterborough was paid ten dollars by the Walpole Society as a reward for recovering William Robinson's horse in 1841. Although thieves were chased and captured, these groups were more effective at deterring crime simply because of the organization's existence.

Horse thief–detecting societies served as the neighborhood watch of their day. Although some of these societies still exist today, they are now essentially social organizations with no crime-fighting function.

THE DEATH OF PRISCILLA HARVEY

Rufus Harvey, born in 1797, was the third generation of that family in Chesterfield, New Hampshire. Rufus married Priscilla Walker in April 1821. The couple had a son the following year, and the family lived on their farm there until the summer of 1837.

It was then that Priscilla caught a cold. She became violently ill with abdominal complications and violent, uncontrollable vomiting. She died on July 9, just two months after her thirty-second birthday. Priscilla was laid to rest in the Harvey lot in Chesterfield's Ware-Joslin Cemetery.

Within a few days, the rumors started. It seemed that several town residents felt that Rufus had murdered Priscilla. The violent, painful abdominal complications probably led them to believe that she had been poisoned.

Rufus was upset by the rumors and could not remain silent. He ran an item in the *New Hampshire Sentinel* that read, in part, as follows: "Soon after the death of my beloved wife I was surprised to hear that reports were in circulation charging me with being the cause of it, and that a petition had been drawn up and signed by several individuals in this town for permission to disinter the body." He then offered to allow a council of impartial physicians to examine the body.

A council of twelve physicians was indeed gathered in Chesterfield. They studied all of the evidence and offered their opinion that Priscilla died as the result of catching a cold and a subsequent bowel complaint and by no other means. Their opinion was also published in the local newspapers.

Rufus remarried one year later and went on with his life in Chesterfield. Although his name was cleared, Rufus's later years must have been sad ones. Not only had he lost his first wife and been accused of her murder by his neighbors, but three of his four children died in a nine-year span, all before Rufus Harvey himself passed away in 1868.

Hillsborough Counterfeiting

Captain Jonathan Carr lived in an attractive Cape Cod house in Hillsborough Lower Village in the 1830s. He was well known in town and served as a captain in the militia. Captain Carr was also a bridge builder, managing the 1840 construction of the old stone arch bridge in Hillsborough that carried his name and probably some of the other bridges in town.

According to local reports, Captain Carr was also involved in another activity for which he is remembered today. At that time, many banks issued their own paper banknotes, and counterfeiting was fairly easy and widely done.

A nineteenth-century dry-laid stone arch bridge in Hillsborough, New Hampshire.

According to local sources, Captain Carr attempted to take advantage of that situation by distributing counterfeit money. Furthermore, several well-known residents agreed to circulate the funds.

Reports also indicate that someone notified the authorities and Carr was taken prisoner on the very day that he was to begin circulating the bogus money. Captain Carr went to trial, was sent to the state prison and spent ten years behind bars.

Some people believe that the 1840 stone arch bridge was partially paid for with counterfeit funds. No matter how the bridge was financed, it survived longer than any of the people involved and has been recognized as one of the finest examples of stone arch bridge construction in the country.

The final chapter in this tale of local counterfeiters was not written until the early twentieth century. At that time, one of Hillsborough's stone arch bridges was removed to be replaced by a new structure. A large amount of counterfeit money was found in a niche in the wall of the bridge when it was torn down.

THE MYSTERIOUS DEATH OF MARTIN AHERN

On the morning of March 25, 1869, the readers of local newspapers were greeted by the following advertisement: "Information wanted: of Martin Ahern, an Irishman, about 40 years old, well-built, straight, full, red face, and weighing about 175lbs. Any information concerning him will be thankfully received by his family." Ahern was an Irish immigrant who had arrived in Keene in 1861, found employment with the Cheshire Railroad and built a home on Island Street.

It seems that on the evening of March 20, several friends of Thomas Boyd, Ahern among them, enjoyed dinner and liquors at Boyd's home on Ashuelot Street after helping him saw a large pile of wood at that address. The men laughed and sang until 2:00 a.m., when they separated and headed to their own residences. Martin Ahern, however, never arrived at his home.

Early the next morning, the night watchman from the railroad shops found Ahern's sawhorse, saw and hat under the railroad bridge near the Faulkner and Colony Mill; there was no sign of Ahern. A search was launched, and spikes were driven into the bed of the canal to intercept a body if it should float to that point.

The disappearance caused quite a commotion in town. The police questioned many people, but nothing more could be learned. On the morning of April 28, six weeks after the mysterious disappearance, Ahern's body was found lodged against the spikes that had been placed in the canal for that purpose.

Ahern's skull was badly fractured, and it was the opinion of coroner Samuel Woodward that Ahern had come to his death by violence at the hands of some unknown person. Public opinion was again aroused, and many felt that the body had not floated to the spikes in the canal but had been placed there by the murderer a short time before it was discovered. Despite the attention attracted to the death due to the unusual circumstances, the mysterious case of Martin Ahern was not solved and remains unsolved today.

The Hancock Fugitive

During the month of December 1902, Hancock, New Hampshire minister Charles H. Chapin and his wife, Myrtie, welcomed Myrtie's sister and her family for a visit at the parsonage on School Street. The visitors, Harriet and Albert "Doc" Ames and their five-year-old daughter Maurine, traveled from their home in Minneapolis and settled in at the parsonage for what they hoped would be a quiet visit.

The Reverend Chapin had married an Acworth girl in 1866 and had worked for a time in Doc Ames's office in Minneapolis before he returned to New Hampshire; he became pastor of the Hancock Congregational Church in 1898.

Doc Ames had a successful medical career and was widely known for supporting the care and rights of Civil War veterans. That support was probably one of the reasons he became involved in politics. Ames was elected mayor of Minneapolis four times between 1876 and 1901. He became more controversial with each passing term, and it soon became clear that his trip to Hancock was not really about rest and relaxation.

The appearance of the January issue of *McClure's* magazine included a scathing article about Doc Ames that caused upheaval in Hancock. Ames had been charged with extortion, conspiracy and bribe taking in Minneapolis, where he jumped bail and forfeited $10,000 in bonds when he left town and failed to appear for trial. It seemed that he began his fourth term as mayor by appointing his brother, Fred, as chief of police. Fred invited a professional gambler to help him with law enforcement. Doc Ames looked the other way when the police took a hands-off approach to the regulation of saloons and gambling halls, which he personally visited often. He was indicted and arraigned in the summer of 1902.

Gossip was rampant in Hancock after the article appeared, and Chapin preached a sermon stating his belief that his brother-in-law was innocent. The authorities were notified, and a county sheriff from Minnesota arrived to arrest Ames. The sheriff said that Ames was "changed almost beyond recognition, broken in spirit and a physical wreck." Furthermore, he had no idea why the sheriff was there. Ames departed from Hancock on the 3:20 p.m. train on March 10, with a large crowd of curious and excited Hancock residents looking on.

He decided not to fight extradition and left the state on March 15 to return to Minneapolis. He was found guilty of bribery and extortion and sentenced to serve six years in the Minnesota penitentiary. His conviction was later thrown out on a technicality, and he was never retried. Ames continued his medical practice until his death in 1911. His funeral was attended by many mourners.

The Reverend Charles Chapin resigned as the minister of the Hancock church at the end of 1903. He took a new post at a church in New Salem, Massachusetts, where he continued to maintain that his brother-in-law, the notorious Doc Ames, was innocent of any crimes.

THE MURDER OF ASAHEL DUNTON

On September 22, 1903, Asahel Dunton died at the Elliot Hospital in Keene from the result of murderous blows that he had received while at the home of Malachi Barnes in Sullivan three days earlier. Dunton worked at a mill in Sullivan and boarded at the Barnes home.

On the evening of the assault, Dunton had aided Mrs. Barnes in digging potatoes. Mr. Barnes appeared angry that Dunton had aided Mrs. Barnes in this chore. Mr. Barnes had previously shown signs of severe jealousy of Dunton.

As darkness arrived, Mrs. Barnes went into the house by the side door. She was immediately attacked by a man who had descended the stairs near her. She was assaulted with a bark peeler but managed to escape and fled to a neighbor's house.

Several men returned to the Barneses' home. Upon their arrival, they found that Dunton, who was lying on a sofa in the house, had been attacked with the bark peeler and was seriously injured. Dunton was taken to the Keene hospital, where he died three days later.

Malachi Barnes denied having any connection with the assault, but he was immediately arrested and held without bail in Keene. It was the opinion of many Sullivan residents that Barnes was mentally unstable and that he had probably committed the crime.

Barnes was tried for murder in January 1904. His lawyers argued that Dunton had been known to keep large sums of money in his room and that the attack may well have been the work of a burglar. Mrs. Barnes was the only witness, and her testimony did not make a strong case against her husband. However, the defense failed to make it appear that any strangers had been near the Barneses' home on the day of the murder. On January 6, the jury brought in a verdict of guilty, and on January 7, Malachi Barnes was sentenced to life imprisonment at the state prison in Concord.

Chapter 9

GONE TO WAR

NEIGHBOR AGAINST NEIGHBOR: A TALE OF THE REVOLUTIONARY WAR

The town of Nelson, New Hampshire, then known as Packersfield, was settled in the mid-1760s. The town's first settler was Breed Batchelder, a surveyor from Massachusetts who made the original survey and first map of the township. Batchelder also owned more than two thousand acres in the town and was accepted as the new community's political and social leader.

By the time the Revolutionary War began, the town had about two hundred residents. Among those were brothers John, Richard and Absalom Farwell. The Farwells arrived soon after Batchelder and developed farms on land that is near the current Silver Lake. When the Revolution began, Batchelder and the Farwells took opposite sides in the conflict. Surveyor Batchelder remained loyal to Great Britain and strongly opposed the call for independence. The Farwells welcomed the break with Britain and strongly supported the Patriot cause.

Batchelder was probably the region's most outspoken Loyalist, berating his neighbors, the New Hampshire government and the new Continental Congress and refusing to serve in the military. Batchelder was threatened with physical harm by his angry neighbors and escaped to hide in a cave for three months. He eventually left town to escape their wrath and went to join the British army to fight against the Patriots.

The Farwell boys all joined the Patriot militia and were probably among the town's residents who marched to Lexington and Concord at the outbreak of the war. Richard and Absalom also signed up to join General John Stark's brigade that marched toward Bennington, Vermont, to intercept British general John Burgoyne's army that marched south from Canada in 1777.

In the resulting Battle of Bennington, Absalom and Richard fought side by side. As the battle raged, Richard stood in the open firing at the British troops. Absalom yelled to him to get down or the enemy would put his daylights out. Amazingly, in the heat of battle, Richard recognized his former neighbor Breed Batchelder across the field of battle. Batchelder was fighting for Burgoyne's British army. Farwell took careful aim and fired. He reported that he was sure he had killed Batchelder, but in fact, he had hit him in the shoulder. It was a serious wound, and Batchelder was sent to Canada with other wounded soldiers. His arm was useless, and he eventually ended up in Nova Scotia, where he reportedly fell out of a boat and was drowned in 1785.

After the Battle of Bennington, militiaman Richard Farwell returned to his Packersfield farm to resume civilian life. He died in 1817 at the age of seventy-four and is buried in the cemetery on the old Nelson town common.

The Six Stevens Sons

Henry Stevens was a farmer near the village of South Stoddard, New Hampshire, during the mid-1800s. Henry and his wife, Hannah, were the parents of ten sons and six daughters. One son died in the early 1850s. The surviving fifteen children ranged in age from six to twenty-seven years old when the Civil War began in 1861.

Henry had served as a captain in the militia, and several of his sons were destined to serve in the military as well. Six of the nine surviving Stevens boys served in the Union army during the war. The military record of these six young men is an amazing tale of patriotism for one family.

George, Daniel and John Stevens, ages seventeen, eighteen and nineteen, were all mustered into the army within one week late in 1861. Anthony and Charles joined five months later. All five of these boys saw action at the front lines. George was shot through the leg at Second Bull Run and rescued by his brother John. John himself avoided injury in several battles but succumbed to disease and was discharged as disabled in 1863. He later reenlisted in the First New Hampshire Cavalry.

Daniel was shot through the mouth at Petersburg. Charles was wounded at the Wilderness and captured by the enemy at the Battle of Spotsylvania.

Anthony was killed at the Battle of Fredericksburg at the age of sixteen. Henry, the sixth son to serve, did not enlist until 1864 because he was needed at home on the farm. He finally did enlist in September of that year. One month later, he died of disease with the army at New York.

Of the six Stevens brothers who served, two died in the war. Three others were wounded, one captured and one discharged because of disease. This Stoddard family's record of patriotism and sacrifice was equaled by few other families during the Civil War.

Elbridge Locke, Songster

Elbridge Locke was born in Stoddard, New Hampshire, on New Year's Day 1818. As a youngster in Stoddard, he sat with aged veterans of the Revolution and listened to their tales of the war. It was here that he learned of the songs sung in military camps and of their importance to the morale of the soldiers.

When the Civil War began in 1861, Locke wanted to enlist in the army, but he could not pass the physical exam because of an injury caused by an accident earlier in life. He volunteered to serve without pay, but his congressman could not find a position for him.

Locke had met Abraham Lincoln some years earlier and decided to travel to Washington to visit the president personally. As he sat in the waiting room at the White House with dozens of other people who had come to ask for jobs, Locke realized how he could be most helpful to the army.

He asked the president's permission to go to the army to sing for the soldiers. Lincoln eagerly accepted the offer. He gave Locke a letter of introduction and a pass to travel to the front and sent him off with the words "God Bless you....Go to the army, and cheer the men around the camp-fires with your songs."

Locke purchased a bedroll, printed sheet music of his songs and went to join the troops. On his first visit to the camps, he was strongly discouraged from singing by several officers and enlisted men. When he began to sing and make jokes, however, several hundred men gathered around and joined in.

Locke spent the next three years traveling with the Armies of the Potomac and the Cumberland, singing in camps and hospitals and writing words and music for new songs. His only income was through the sale of sheet music to the troops; the men shared their food and shelter with him.

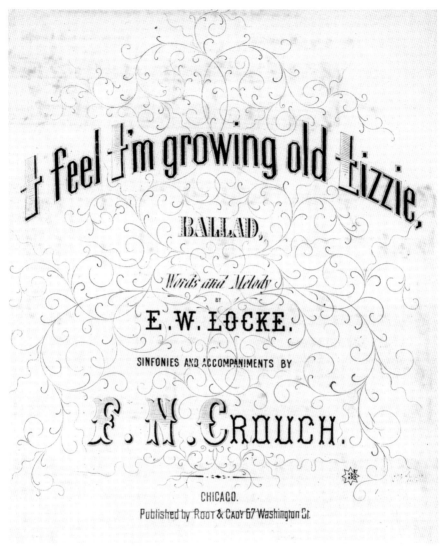

Sheet music for the song "I Feel I'm Growing Old Lizzie," written by Civil War musician Elbridge Locke.

Locke's music was soon published by a company in New York, and his name became known far and wide as Americans everywhere sang the patriotic songs of Stoddard's Elbridge Locke.

YANKEE SPY

Jonathan D. Hale was born on a small farm in Stoddard, New Hampshire, in July 1817. He grew up in the town before traveling far away to seek his fortune. Jonathan and his brother Obed became teachers as their father had been before them. In the late 1830s, they left Stoddard and traveled south and west into Kentucky. They taught at several schools and academies as they worked their way south. Obed soon married, and Jonathan traveled on alone.

He continued into northern Tennessee, where he taught English and penmanship. In December 1843, he married one of his students, Pheroba Chilton. Pheroba was a wealthy heiress, and Jonathan and Pheroba spent the next eighteen years building a mill village on her land on the Wolf River. By 1860, they were comfortably situated there with a village named for them, Hales Mills, and a growing family.

When the Civil War began, Jonathan, being a New Hampshire native, offered his services to Union military officials. He knew the geography of north central Tennessee so well that he was soon appointed captain and chief of scouts of the Union Army of the Cumberland. For the next four years, he was away from his family spying on Confederate armies, making maps, gathering food and horses, guiding troops to the front and carrying out a wide variety of other duties to assist the Union. He was rarely paid for his services.

Being a spy was a dangerous occupation. On two occasions, he was almost executed, once after being captured and once by a band of marauding Confederate guerrillas. Furthermore, the entire village of Hales Mills, Tennessee, was burned to the ground by Confederates because of his support for the Union. The Hale family lost everything in the war but decided to return to Hales Mills and rebuild after the fighting ended. The building was progressing nicely when a new enemy appeared. In the late 1860s, Jonathan began to receive threats from the Ku Klux Klan because he treated Blacks well and because of his role in the trial of a Confederate guerrilla who was executed for war crimes.

Jonathan and his family fled Tennessee in 1869 after the Klan attempted to murder him. Hales Mills was burned once again, and he brought his destitute family to his hometown of Stoddard. Although Jonathan Hale led a life of adventure, wealth, heartbreak and poverty in distant states, he passed away in a small farmhouse overlooking Center Pond in Stoddard in 1896, one and a half miles from where he was born.

Jonathan Davis Hale, captain and chief of scouts of the Army of the Cumberland, poses with his rifle and field glasses.

Webber Family Sacrifice

Conrad Webber was born in Switzerland in 1812. Conrad; his wife, Mary; and their three children left their home in Switzerland at the end of 1850 to come to the United States. Mary was ill, and her doctor advised her to take a sea voyage. Consequently, the family sailed to America and settled in Ellenville, New York. They remained there for a year and a half before being offered jobs at the Granite Glass Company in Stoddard. The Webbers moved to Stoddard, where they were employed weaving rattan onto the larger bottles produced at the glass factory.

Conrad and Mary had two daughters, Elizabeth and Barbara, and a son, Conrad Jr. The 1860 census listed Conrad and Mary, both age forty-nine; Conrad Jr., age eighteen; and Barbara, age fourteen, as members of the Webber household. Daughter Elizabeth had already married and left home. Conrad, Mary and Conrad Jr. were all employed "willowing bottles."

The Webbers purchased sixty acres of land near Island Pond and began to build a house. The house was not complete when the Civil War began. Conrad Jr. enlisted in Company H of the Second Regiment of New Hampshire Volunteers on September 21, 1861, as a private. Despite his age, Conrad Sr. also enlisted. He signed up with twelve other Stoddard residents in Company G of the Fourteenth Regiment of New Hampshire Volunteers in August 1862.

Mary and Barbara stayed at home in Stoddard. On one occasion, Elizabeth came to visit and found her mother quite ill. It was winter, and it had been snowing. Elizabeth shoveled a trail more than 850 feet through the snow so the doctor could get to the house.

Conrad Jr., with his regiment in Virginia, ate poisoned food left by the Confederates and fell ill. He died as a result of the poisoning in camp at Falmouth, Virginia, on February 8, 1863. Just two weeks later, the regiment returned home to New Hampshire.

Conrad Sr. was taken prisoner by the Confederate army at the Battle of Cedar Creek on October 19, 1864. He died of disease two months later, on December 13, at the Confederate prison in Salisbury, North Carolina. Conrad Sr. and Conrad Jr. were both buried in the South where they died, but their family erected a gravestone for them in Stoddard. Conrad Sr. was fifty-two years of age at the time of his death; Conrad Jr. was twenty years old. These two recent immigrants to the United States died fighting for their new home country.

Mary Webber applied for a widow's pension after Conrad's death and was awarded eight dollars per month. She did not have much time to make use

Fifty-year-old Conrad Webber in his Civil War uniform, 1862.

of the pension, however. She suffered from severe depression after her son and husband died. Mary was sent to the state asylum at Concord where she died on February 19, 1867, age 54. Daughter Barbara married Henry A. Tyrrell of Stoddard in March 1864. They moved to Maine, where she lived to age 104.

World War Hero James Butler

James S. Butler was born in Stoddard, New Hampshire, in 1896. His family soon moved to Keene, where he attended grammar and high school. At age sixteen, he enlisted in the coast artillery but was soon discharged when his true age was discovered. He then joined the New Hampshire Militia and served in the Mexican border conflict.

Butler quickly enlisted when the call came for U.S. soldiers to serve in World War I. He was among the first troops to ship out to France. Butler's actions and leadership soon resulted in his promotion to sergeant and then his transfer to the intelligence section of his regiment.

This Keene soldier was soon receiving commendations for his actions on the field. On one occasion, he led a unit out to determine the enemy's position. Because he did not want to endanger his men, he advanced without them across the battlefield until fired on by enemy machine guns, thereby exposing their position. Another time, he swam across a river in France and entered the German headquarters there to gather valuable information for his commanders. When the task was completed, he headed back toward the river. He was discovered when he crawled out of the enemy trenches and was attacked by twelve German soldiers. He killed two with his rifle, which then jammed. Butler then dispatched two more with his pistol. His aggressive tactics so shocked the Germans that they turned and fled. Butler made his way back across the river and delivered the information.

He was awarded the Distinguished Service Cross by General Pershing, as well as the French Croix de Guerre. James Butler also received several other medals for his actions in the conflict. He returned home to Keene after the war, where he was hailed as a hero. The modest young man was called upon to make speeches across New Hampshire and Vermont. Unfortunately, Butler had been severely gassed during his time in the trenches. The damage to his lungs proved too severe, and he passed away at age twenty-four in June 1920.

Thousands of people attended his funeral in Keene, filling St. Bernard's Catholic Church and the street out front. Inside the church, his comrades recognized the service, leadership and sacrifice of World War I hero James S. Butler.

Chapter 10

ANIMALS AND NATURE

THE BEAR IN THE BOAT

Local legend indicates that during the mid-1700s, a hunter by the name of Spafford lived near the shore of the lake in Chesterfield. This was before permanent settlers came to the town, and it is said that the lake, now known as Spofford Lake, was named for this early hunter. John and Silas Spafford were early proprietors of the town; perhaps he was related to one of those men.

One story about hunter Spafford tells of his experiences one day while fishing in the lake. It seems that he was out in a small flat-bottomed boat when he saw an animal begin to swim across the lake. Spafford rowed closer to investigate and found that the animal was a large bear. He tried to shoot the bear, but his musket had gotten wet while lying on the floor of the boat and would not fire.

The bear promptly changed course, swam to the boat and climbed in, nearly tipping the boat in the process. Spafford was about to club the bear with his musket when it shook the water from its fur and sat down in the front of the boat, paying no attention to Spafford in the rear.

Spafford quietly turned the boat and started to row toward the near shore from which the bear had started. When the boat was headed in that direction, however, the bear turned on Spafford, bared its teeth and growled loudly. Spafford tried this tactic two or three times, but each time, the bear growled at him. The hunter found that the bear remained quiet if the boat was headed toward the opposite shore. Spafford continued in that direction, and the bear remained content.

The legend indicates that when the boat reached shallow water, it jumped overboard and swam to shore. Spafford was relieved to see the bear disappear into the woods. It is said that Spafford never tired of sharing with his grandchildren the story of his experience paddling a bear across Spofford Lake.

HORATIO THE ELEPHANT

The first elephant brought to Cheshire County was displayed at the Ralston Tavern in Keene in 1815. It was five years before another elephant was brought through the region to be exhibited to the local residents. This second elephant, named Horatio, had been imported to America by Captain Abraham Roblin of New York.

While exhibiting the elephant in Vermont, Captain Roblin sold him in Woodstock to three Vermonters. The new owners had difficulty with the animal, however, and Roblin agreed to travel with them until he was satisfied that they could control Horatio. On the evening of September 19, 1820, the exhibition left Putney, Vermont, on its way to Keene for another show and then planned to go on toward Boston, where the elephant would be exhibited through the winter.

Elephants were often moved at night then to avoid giving residents a free show. The group arrived at the bridge connecting Putney with Westmoreland, New Hampshire, across the Connecticut River. The bridge there was 24 feet wide and 430 feet long. It was a toll bridge, and there was a delay in getting the gate opened; the group finally began to cross around midnight. Horatio did not want to cross, so two attendants on horseback rode in front and two others, including Captain Roblin, rode behind to urge the animal across the bridge. The group was just arriving at the Westmoreland side when a defective cross-timber gave way under the elephant's weight. Horatio, Captain Roblin and the other attendant in the rear all plunged through the bridge and onto the rocks about 40 feet below. The two horses were killed instantly, Roblin's thigh was broken and his head and spine badly injured. The second attendant's leg was shattered.

One of the men with the party rode to Keene to get Dr. Amos Twitchell to come and treat those who were injured. He arrived four hours after the accident and just a few minutes before Captain Roblin died of his injuries.

The other man's leg was so badly injured that Dr. Twitchell had to amputate. Horatio was still on the rocks and could not move. A block and tackle were set up to get him on his feet, but it was discovered that his back was probably broken, and he could not stand.

Local residents eventually got the elephant onto an ox sled, and eight yokes of oxen pulled him up the embankment to a barn in Westmoreland. Folks from the neighborhood cared for him, but Horatio died one week later. The elephant was buried there in Westmoreland, but not before his skin was sent to Boston, where it was displayed for years at the Boston Museum.

The bridge was rebuilt after its collapse, only to be destroyed by a flood about a decade later. It was not replaced this time, but the spot became the site of Britton's Ferry so that travelers could still cross the river there by boat. Horatio and the so-called Elephant Bridge have not been forgotten, but the only evidence there of the story are the bridge abutments and the remains of the bridge, which still lie in the bottom of the Connecticut River.

In the Lion's Cage

John Sears, the son of a cobbler, was born in Keene in the late 1790s. During the early 1800s, an impressive animal show visited Keene. Sears was fascinated by the show and asked the manager, Mr. Page, many questions about the animals. Page was impressed with young John Sears and planned with the boy's mother for him to work with the animal show through the summer.

He worked well with the animals and decided not to return home at the end of the season, except to give his mother most of his wages. Sears continued to work with animal shows and soon became a nationally known animal trainer, working especially well with large animals. He became famous for his ability to easily gain favor with the animals that were part of the menagerie.

He founded the New England Caravan in 1830. In the mid-1830s, he brought his caravan of wild animals to Keene. The creatures were exhibited under a large tent and created a local sensation. Sears later operated the Great Eastern Menagerie, which performed throughout the New England states. The show was billed as having sixty living wild animals that were displayed under a 120-foot-long tent.

On one occasion, the showman consented to being shut up in a room with a savage bear before he purchased it to determine if it could be trained. An intense confrontation ensued, but Sears won the confrontation, bought the bear and taught it to do a variety of tricks. At one time, he lost his entire collection of animals, valued at $10,000, to a fire in Boston. He rebuilt his show, however, and remained in the business until the end of his life.

Sears's greatest claim to fame was the fact that he was the first person in this country to enter a lion's cage. In about 1827, he snuck into a lion's cage and sat for a while on the animal's back. He regularly entered cages with lions thereafter.

Keene native and animal tamer John Sears was one of the foremost showmen in the country at the time of his death. He passed away in 1875 at the age of seventy-six. His death was caused by an infection that resulted from a bite from a baboon in his animal collection.

GALEN CLARK IN THE WILDERNESS

Jonas Clark settled in Dublin, New Hampshire, in the year 1797. He operated a woolen mill there until 1804, when he moved with his wife and four young children to the wilderness of Shipton, Quebec. The Clarks had seven more children after their move to Canada. Their seventh child, Galen, was born in Shipton in March 1814.

The Clark family returned to Dublin in 1819, and it was here that Galen spent his childhood years. He tried his hand at farming as a young man but did not care for that profession and moved to Missouri in the 1830s. He married Rebecca McCoy in 1839, and the couple moved to Philadelphia. Rebecca died there, and he drifted westward and prospected for gold in California. While in California, Clark's health failed, and the doctors he conferred with gave him about one year to live.

Discouraged, he hiked alone into the Sierra Nevada Mountains. While hunting near Yosemite Valley, Clark met a group of Indians who told him a fabulous tale of a forest of gigantic trees that no white man had ever seen. He investigated their tale and was amazed to find himself among a growth of evergreens averaging more than 250 feet tall and 20 feet in diameter. Clark had found California's giant sequoia redwood trees. He remained among these trees, regained his health, opened a small hotel nearby and began a guide service to teach others about the amazing trees.

Clark encouraged the protection of the trees and received support from Congress. The Yosemite Grant was signed into law in 1864, and the land was turned over to the State of California to be used by the public for resort and recreation. In 1890, the federal government created Yosemite National Park, encompassing Yosemite Valley and the Mariposa Grove of Giant Sequoias. In 1866, former Dublin, New Hampshire farm boy Galen Clark was appointed official guardian and custodian of the park and the forest, a position he held for twenty-four years.

Chapter 11

DANGER AND DISASTER

The Great Walpole Fire

Shortly after midnight on Friday, September 17, 1849, the village of Walpole was aroused by the cry of "fire!" The large, long three-story brick business block that housed Philip Peck's dry goods and grocery store in the center of the village was ablaze. Peck's store was quickly consumed before the fire broke through the shutters and spread to the other stores in the building. Another grocery store and a variety shop on the first floor were also destroyed.

The town's only fire engine was under repair at the time and could not be used. As a result, the entire brick block and most of its contents were lost, including a lawyer's office and other offices on the second floor of the building. The lack of fire apparatus also meant that the buildings nearby could not be protected. The fire spread to the building immediately to the west, and then the next building, and the next.

Two of these buildings contained a grocery store, a milliner's shop and a shoe shop; the third was a residence. The owners of these buildings had enough warning to remove some of their stock, personal belongings and furniture before the fire became too hot.

The Bellows residence nearby was also threatened with destruction until Mr. Titus of Keene arrived and told Mrs. Bellows that he could save her house if allowed to lead the effort. He quickly cut a hole in the roof and directed the Bellows family and their neighbors to carry water to the attic and pour it over the roof and the side of the house. The best parlor carpet was also placed on the roof to protect it from embers.

Around 6:00 a.m., the fire began to abate. The four buildings that had caught fire were destroyed. The Bellowses' fences were dilapidated, the yard full of bricks, the fruit trees damaged, the grass destroyed and their belongings spread across the village, but their house had been saved, thanks to Mr. Titus.

The financial losses were considerable, as was the commercial loss to the town. The cause of the "great fire of Walpole" was never determined. After the fire, all the property was purchased by John Cole. He quickly replaced the old business block with two new store buildings, as well as a grocery store and dwelling where the three buildings to the west had burned. Just five years later, an overheated stovepipe caused a fire in the new dwelling. This time, the fire spread to the east, destroying all the new buildings and laying waste once again to the previously burned-over commercial section of Walpole village.

The Hurricane of 1854

One of the worst windstorms on record for Keene was what local residents called the "Hurricane of 1854." The storm occurred late in the season, on December 3, and was combined with a fierce snowstorm. The wind began at four o'clock on a Sunday afternoon with the snow starting to fall at the same time. The wind increased persistently and blew violently until after midnight. People feared that their homes would be destroyed as the buildings groaned and swayed in the wind.

According to local newspaper accounts, more than a dozen Keene barns were destroyed or lost their roofs. Several homes and bridges were severely damaged, and fifty chimneys were blown over in the town. The roof of the Ashuelot Railroad covered bridge over the Ashuelot River was demolished.

Thousands of trees were laid flat by the wind. Stephen Chase lost six hundred old-growth pine trees on his land near the Ashuelot River. He built a sawmill the following spring to cut the timber. John Albee built a second new mill near Woodburn Street to handle the large amount of timber blown down by the storm.

One of the timber lots most severely damaged was the Dinsmoor Woods along the Five Mile Drive, now Maple Avenue. The Dinsmoor Woods were destined to be destroyed again more than eighty years later by the hurricane of 1938.

These winds, which reached hurricane proportions in some areas, were a damaging blow to our ancestors. Along with the gale, however, fifteen to eighteen inches of snow fell in Keene, leaving roads and railways impassable for days and making repairs very difficult. This storm was remembered and discussed by generations of Keene residents until the devastating hurricane of 1938 overshadowed the hurricane of 1854.

THE FLOOD OF 1869

One of the worst floods in the history of southwestern New Hampshire inundated the region in October 1869. Rain began to fall in Cheshire County on Saturday night, October 2. It continued through Sunday, by which time more than two inches had fallen. Then, on Monday, October 4, the deluge began. Almost five and a half inches of rain fell on that day, four inches of it between 12:30 and 2:30 p.m. Almost seven and a half inches fell during the three-day period.

The water level in local brooks and rivers was dangerously high by the afternoon of October 4. Highways and bridges began to disappear into the turbulent waters. Railroad lines were washed out in several locations, and trains could not run. Highways in Keene sustained more than $4,000 in damages, which would be about $90,000 today. The loss in Marlborough was even greater.

Buildings along the Ashuelot River and Beaver Brook in Keene sustained heavy damage, but Brattleboro was especially hard hit. Several major bridges on Whetstone Brook and the Connecticut River were destroyed. Businesses and homes along the brook were also destroyed, some of them before the residents could escape. A total of $300,000 in damage was sustained in Brattleboro, and two people lost their lives in the floodwaters there. Special trains were run from Keene to North Walpole so that the passengers could see the water flowing over Bellows Falls.

Potato and corn crops were destroyed, and Jonathan Robinson of Keene lost thirty-six sheep in the flood. The Troy Blanket Mills factory was undermined, and the lower level of the building was a complete loss. Charles Bingham had just finished building his new house on the banks of Mill Brook in Gilsum. His furniture was moved in, but not his family. Bingham was sleeping in his new home on the night of October 4 and barely managed to escape through a bedroom window as his house and possessions were washed away by the floodwaters. Although the damage was immense throughout the region, no lives were lost in Cheshire County during the famous flood of October 1869.

The Resort Hotel without Any Guests

The Mount Huggins Hotel in the town of Swanzey was the dream of Emma Knapp of Haverhill, Massachusetts. Knapp hired two Keene contractors to build the hotel in 1883. It was located on a seventy-five-acre lot on the 1,021-foot-tall Mount Huggins in the northeast corner of Swanzey, across Route 12 from the current site of the Cheshire Fairgrounds.

The hotel was an impressive building, similar to the grand hotels of the White Mountain of the same period. The structure was 96 by 142 feet in size and four stories high. The hotel was built of wood with a French mansard roof. The dining room, located on the second floor, seated one hundred people. There was also a ballroom on the fourth floor. The building was equipped with a steam-operated passenger elevator. Tennis courts and other recreation facilities were planned for the hotel grounds.

The owner experienced financial difficulties before the building could be completed, however, and the courts gave possession of the property to the contractors in 1885. Morgan Sherman, the proprietor of Keene's famous Cheshire House hotel, purchased the Mount Huggins Hotel. Sherman completed the construction and began to furnish the hotel late in 1887, preparing to open the facility to summer visitors the following June. Much of the furniture had been put in place by the beginning of 1888.

At about 10:30 p.m. on the night of January 11 of that year, the engineer of the late train from Boston reported that he had seen a fire in the building as the train passed through Swanzey. Sherman rushed to the scene with an acquaintance, and the Keene Fire Department was notified. Sherman and his friend were the first to arrive at the scene.

They tried to enter through the front door but were driven back by the smoke and flames. They entered the north end of the building and were able to remove some of the furniture, but the building was soon fully engulfed in flames. The fire department could not save it. By morning, the five-year-old Mount Huggins Hotel was completely destroyed, without having sheltered one guest within its elegant walls.

VIOLENT WINDS

When we think of the famous hurricane of 1938, we are reminded of the great devastation that the storm caused in the Monadnock region. Although that storm probably received the most publicity and media coverage of any storm to hit our area, the annals of local history are filled with reports of other violent hurricanes and tornados that visited the region.

Several hurricanes caused considerable damage in our vicinity during the early 1800s. A tornado during 1807 destroyed several buildings in downtown Keene. Another tornado cut a swath through the town of Antrim, toppling trees, flipping automobiles, destroying barns and damaging homes in 1922.

The "Great Gale" of July 1877 swept through Gilsum, Sullivan and Nelson, flattening wood lots, sending carriages flying through the air and moving several houses from their foundations. The storm destroyed eleven barns, two sugarhouses and three apple orchards. In Gilsum, it lifted the district #3 schoolhouse, turned it around ninety degrees and placed it back on the ground without damaging the plaster on the walls. The

The tornado of 1922 damaged several buildings and automobiles in Antrim, including the McIlvin house, shown here.

wind lifted two people into the air and placed them down again uninjured. The whirlwind came and went within two minutes; it blew itself out after passing into the town of Hancock.

Perhaps the most violent storm prior to 1938, however, was the hurricane of August 19, 1788. This storm had a narrow path but was intense in our area. The local newspaper reported that the damage to houses, barns and cattle was beyond conception. Although no people lost their lives to these violent winds, more than one hundred cows were killed by falling trees during the hurricane of 1788.

BIBLIOGRAPHY

Allison, Henry Darracott. *Dublin Days Old and New*. New York: Exposition Press, 1952.

Bowditch, Henry I. *Memoir of Amos Twitchell, M.D.* Boston: John Wilson and Son, 1852.

Buss, Daniel. *Genealogy of the Buss Family and Their Descendants*. Keene, NH: privately printed, 1888.

Cheshire County Chap-Book: Notes, Antiquities, History. Keene, NH: Historical Society of Cheshire County, 1965.

Cheshire Republican. Keene, NH, 1878–1909.

Cummings, Silas, Account Book, 1827–1829. Historical Society of Cheshire County, Keene, NH.

Eliason, Robert E. *Graves & Company Musical Instrument Makers*. Dearborn, MI: Greenfield Village & Henry Ford Museum, 1975.

Frizzell, Martha McDonalds. *A History of Walpole, New Hampshire*. Walpole, NH: Walpole Historical Society, 1963.

Fuller, Robert. *Jubilee Jim, from Circus Traveler to Wall Street Rogue*. New York: Texere, 2012.

Griffin, Simon G. *A History of the Town of Keene from 1732, When the Township Was Granted by Massachusetts, to 1874, When It Became a City*. Keene, NH: Sentinel Printing, 1904.

Hale, Salma. *Annals of the Town of Keene, from Its First Settlement, in 1735, to the Year 1790*. Keene, NH: J.W. Prentiss and Company, 1851.

The Historical Society of Temple. *A History of Temple New Hampshire, 1768–1976*. Dublin, NH: William L. Bauhan, 1976.

The History Committee of the Stoddard Historical Society. *The History of the Town of Stoddard, New Hampshire.* Stoddard, NH: Stoddard Historical Society, 1974.

Keene History Committee. *"Upper Ashuelot": A History of Keene, New Hampshire.* Keene, NH: City of Keene, 1968.

Locke, Elbridge W. *Three Years in Camp and Hospital.* Boston: Geo. D. Russell & Co., 1870.

Marlborough Recollections Being a Gathering of Myths & Tales and an Accounting of Cellar Holes, Abandoned Sites & Moved Buildings in Marlborough, New Hampshire. Marlborough, NH: Marlborough Historical Society, 1986.

Messenger, Edward Marshall. *A Simple Life of Three-Score Ten.* Winchester, MA: Winchester Star, 1911.

New Hampshire Recorder. Keene, NH, November 1787.

New Hampshire Sentinel. Keene, NH, 1799–1910.

Norton, John F. *The History of Fitzwilliam, New Hampshire, from 1752–1887.* New York: Burr Printing House, 1888.

Springfield Manufacturing Company, Manufacturers of Springfield Portable Houses. Keene, NH. Springfield Manufacturing Company, 1912, (1914).

Vermont Phoenix. Brattleboro, VT, January 4, 1918.

Waterbury, Jean Parker. *Laban Ainsworth: A Life.* Jaffrey, NH: Jaffrey Historical Society, 2019.

ABOUT THE AUTHOR

Alan Rumrill is a native of the Monadnock region, where his family has lived since 1770. He has been executive director of the Historical Society of Cheshire County for thirty-nine years. During that time, he has written eight books and presented more than one thousand programs on the region's history and art. He also prepares three weekly radio and newspaper features on local history.

Visit us at
www.historypress.com